Making Sure of Maths
Book 3

T. F. Watson, M.A., F.E.I.S. and T. A. Quinn, M.A.

Metric Edition

Published by Holmes McDougall Limited, Edinburgh
Printed by George Outram and Company Limited, Perth
Designed by Bob Crawford
Copyright © Holmes McDougall Limited, 1970
SBN 7157 0752–3

Contents

Looking Back

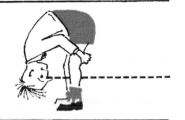

A What number is:

	(a)	(b)	(c)	(d)
1.	5 more than 26?	6 less than 20?	10 less than 42?	15 more than 70?
2.	9 more than 35?	7 less than 25?	20 less than 93?	25 more than 80?
3.	7 more than 43?	8 less than 36?	20 less than 110?	25 less than 100?
4.	8 more than 45?	9 less than 32?	30 less than 120?	25 more than 90?
5.	9 more than 57?	5 less than 31?	40 less than 130?	35 more than 80?

6. Write the numbers shown by these pictures:

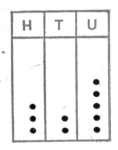 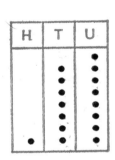 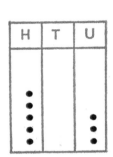 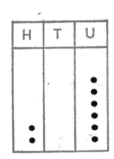 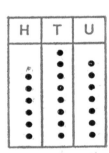

7. Draw pictures adding 18 to each of the numbers above.

8. How many tens are there in:
   (a) 90?   (b) 110?   (c) 195?   (d) 206?   (e) 350?

9. How many hundreds are there in:
   (a) 926?   (b) 1 000?   (c) 3 900?   (d) 7 600?   (e) 8 200?

B Write the answers only:

	(a)	(b)	(c)	(d)	(e)
1.	15 × 10	5 × 100	70 ÷ 10	900 ÷ 100	200 ÷ 50
2.	36 × 10	9 × 100	100 ÷ 10	1 200 ÷ 100	500 ÷ 50
3.	97 × 10	12 × 100	120 ÷ 10	2 000 ÷ 100	450 ÷ 50
4.	58 × 10	25 × 100	250 ÷ 10	3 100 ÷ 100	1 000 ÷ 50

5

5. Write these in figures:

   (a) One hundred and forty.
   (b) Three hundred and ninety-five.
   (c) Six hundred and thirty-two.
   (d) One thousand three hundred and fifty.
   (e) Thirty thousand.
   (f) Seven thousand two hundred and seventy-six.
   (g) Forty two thousand nine hundred and eighty-three.
   (h) Fifty six thousand four hundred and seven.
   (j) Eighty thousand seven hundred.
   (k) Ninety thousand and fifty two.

6. Read these numbers aloud to your teacher:

415	2 300	12 468	317 261	300 100
270	3 467	14 930	428 320	240 099
509	5 250	23 609	153 036	702 050

7. Write these numbers in words:

| 274 | 3 195 | 20 000 | 100 000 | 32 050 |
| 460 | 4 270 | 14 370 | 120 500 | 114 206 |

8. Make the biggest possible number, using all these figures:

   (a) 4, 1, 8   (b) 3, 0, 4   (c) 2, 6, 0, 5   (d) 4, 9, 1, 7

9. Write the smallest possible number, using all these figures:

   (a) 5, 9, 1   (b) 9, 0, 2   (c) 6, 1, 5, 8   (d) 7, 4, 1, 3

10.

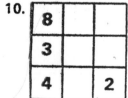 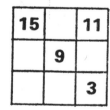 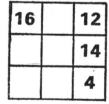 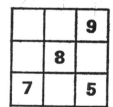

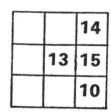

Draw these magic squares in your squared paper exercise book, and fill in the missing numbers. Each row, each column, and each diagonal, should add up to the same total.

6

1. If Jack had 36 more foreign stamps, he would have 150. How many has he?

2. A cinema can hold 850 people. If there are 643 in it, how many more can it hold?

3. There are 286 boys in a school and 259 girls. How many children are there altogether?

4. When a train arrived in York there were 182 people on it. 43 left the train and 73 joined it. How many passengers were there now on the train?

5. There were 7 892 men at a football match. How many was this less than 9 000?

6. A factory employs 2 150 men. 184 travel by car, 389 by bus, and the rest walk. How many walk?

7. 420 children attend Woodend School. One day 43 were absent. How many were present?

8. The population of Lanark is 8 436. The population of Largs is 9 150. How many fewer people live in Lanark than in Largs?

9. The population of Sandgate at the beginning of last year was 12 685. During the year, 129 people died, 348 left the town, and 267 came in. What was the population at the end of the year?

10. 3 450 people watched a cricket match. 2 145 were men, 138 were boys and the rest were women. How many women?

11. I thought of a number. I added 56 to it. The answer was 250. What was the number I thought of?

1. Add:

(a) 46
903
29
276

(b) 238
87
520
109

(c) 473
820
94
207

(d) 196
342
200
475

(e) 358
109
326
417

(f) $307 + 56 + 300$

(g) $25 + 150 + 236$

(h) $238 + 9 + 75$

2. Subtract the following. Check by adding the answer to the bottom line—they should add up to the top line.

(a) 92
-35

(b) 100
-42

(c) 251
-38

(d) 360
-173

(e) 2 753
-435

(f) 41
-17

(g) 150
-35

(h) 215
-86

(j) 4 720
$-2 173$

(k) 5 000
$-2 328$

(l) 83
-47

(m) 200
-73

(n) 323
-185

(o) 3 500
$-1 624$

(p) 4 274
$-2 376$

7

E

(a)	(b)	(c)
1. $(6 \times 3) + (10 \times 5)$	$(8 \times 10) - (5 \times 6)$	$(40 \div 4) + (20 \div 5)$
2. $(5 \times 8) + (7 \times 6)$	$(9 \times 6) - (7 \times 5)$	$(45 \div 5) + (42 \div 7)$
3. $(10 \times 8) + (4 \times 5)$	$(7 \times 7) - (6 \times 6)$	$(7 \times 3) + (3 \times 9)$
4. $(11 \times 6) - (6 \times 4)$	$(9 \times 9) - (9 \times 4)$	$(72 \div 8) - (45 \div 9)$
5. $(5 \times 5) + (9 \times 5)$	$(7 \times 8) + (4 \times 9)$	$(54 \div 6) - (21 \div 7)$
6. $(10 \times 7) - (5 \times 8)$	$(9 \times 4) + (8 \times 3)$	$(100 \div 10) + (40 \div 8)$

7. Find the missing sign (+ or −)

   (a) $9\ ?\ 8 = 12\ ?\ 5$

   (b) $8\ ?\ 7 = 6\ ?\ 9$

   (c) $10\ ?\ 6 = 8\ ?\ 8$

   (d) $2\ ?\ 5 = 10\ ?\ 3$

   (e) $6\ ?\ 4 = 30\ ?\ 20$

   (f) $7\ ?\ 9 = 20\ ?\ 4$

8. Find the missing sign (× or ÷)

   (a) $6\ ?\ 6 = 9\ ?\ 4$

   (b) $32\ ?\ 8 = 12\ ?\ 3$

   (c) $6\ ?\ 5 = 10\ ?\ 3$

   (d) $30\ ?\ 6 = 25\ ?\ 5$

   (e) $5\ ?\ 4 = 60\ ?\ 3$

   (f) $80\ ?\ 4 = 5\ ?\ 4$

9. In each of the following sets three numbers do not belong to the set. Pick them out and put in their place numbers which belong to the set.

   (a) {12, 16, 21, 36, 42, 49} = numbers that divide evenly by 4.

   (b) {10, 15, 22, 30, 36, 42} = numbers that divide evenly by 5.

   (c) {12, 18, 25, 32, 36, 40} = numbers that divide evenly by 6.

   (d) {16, 24, 30, 40, 46, 52} = numbers that divide evenly by 8.

   (e) { 7, 14, 22, 28, 36, 45} = numbers that divide evenly by 7.

10. Find:

   (a) $\frac{1}{2}$ of 38, 56, 72, 96, 26

   (b) $\frac{1}{4}$ of 32, 48, 52, 76, 96

   (c) $\frac{1}{8}$ of 24, 40, 56, 72, 96

   (d) $\frac{1}{6}$ of 36, 48, 60, 72, 90

   (e) $\frac{1}{5}$ of 45, 60, 70, 85, 100

   (f) $\frac{1}{3}$ of 27, 36, 45, 54, 75

   (g) $\frac{1}{7}$ of 21, 42, 63, 77, 84

11. Find the next two numbers in each series:

   (a)   6, 10, 14, 18, ..., ..

   (b) 20, 17, 14, 11, ..., ..

   (c)   2, 10, 18, 26, ..., ..

   (d) 50, 45, 40, 35, ..., ..

   (e)   1, 3, 6, 10, ..., ..

   (f)   5, 6, 8, 11, ..., ..

   (g) 40, 36, 32, 28, ..., ..

F Draw and complete these crosswords. To help you, *a* and *b* in the first crossword have been filled in.

1.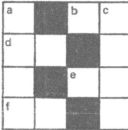

$\begin{array}{ccc}\text{a}&\text{b}&\text{c}\\ 1 & 4 & 4\end{array}$	

Across

a 12×12

d $(25 \times 10) - 4$

g $(10 \times 10 \times 10) - 62$

Down

b $3\frac{1}{2}$ dozen

c 4×11

e $(8 \times 9) - (4 \times 3)$

f 7^2

2.

Across

b $34 + 28 + 16$

d $10^2 - 5^2$

e   6 dozen

f $270 \div 5$

Down

a $5\,000 - 215$

c $(912 \times 4) + (896 \times 5)$

3. *Across*

a 75×5

e $(12 \times 6) - (9 \times 5)$

f $10^2 - 12$

h $(93 \times 6) + (33 \times 5)$

Down

b   6 dozen

c $1\,000 - 422$

d $(19 \times 20) - (31 \times 3)$

g $9^2 + 1$

4. *Across*

a $(15 \times 5) + 3$

c $2\,000 - 246$

e $8^2 - 2$

f 95×5

Down

a 11×7

b $9\,000 - 435$

c $4 \times 3 \times 6 \times 2$

d $7^2 - 7$

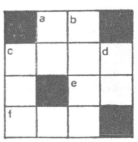

G

	Population	Km from Edinburgh		Population	Km from Edinburgh
Aberfeldy	1 415	114	Crieff	5 773	77
Aberdour	2 000	27	Dunoon	9 437	193
Aberfoyle	1 458	90	Dunbar	3 926	45
Annan	5 696	127	Forres	4 828	259
Banff	3 233	269	Girvan	6 020	150
Braemar	1 018	150	Gourock	9 875	111

The list above gives the population of 12 small towns in Scotland and the number of km from Edinburgh.

1. Arrange these places in order of size, beginning with the largest town. Write the population of each to the nearest hundred.
2. How many more people live in Aberdour than in Aberfeldy?
3. How many more live in Crieff than in Dunbar?
4. About how many times is Gourock the size of Braemar?
5. If 250 people leave Forres and go to live in Banff, how many people would there be in each town?
6. If 125 people leave Girvan and 96 move in, what will its population be then?
7. Which place is furthest from Edinburgh?
8. How many km is Braemar nearer to Edinburgh than is Dunoon?
9. How many km is Gourock nearer to Edinburgh than is Banff?
10. A motorist travelled from Aberfoyle to Edinburgh and then from Edinburgh to Banff. How many km was this?

H Copy this number crossword into your exercise book. Using the clues, fill in the missing numbers.

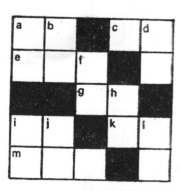

Across

a $\frac{1}{4}$ of 64

c $48 \div 4$

e $(6 \times 20) + 4$

g $3^2 \times 6$

i $(5 \times 8) - 5$

k $(23 \times 2) \times 2$

m 20×30

Down

a $\frac{1}{8}$ of 88

b $(10 \times 5) + (4 \times 3)$

d $(5 \times 10) - (2 \times 11)$

f $3^2 \times 5$

h 7^2

i $(25 \times 2) - (7 \times 2)$

j $\frac{1}{2}$ of 100

l $72 \div 3$

Multiplication and Division

You already know that to multiply by 10 we add a zero to the right,
and to multiply by 20, 30, 40, we multiply by 2, 3, 4, and add a zero.

$$27 \times 10 = 270 \qquad 43 \times 20 = 860 \qquad 35 \times 40 = 1\,400$$

In the same way to multiply by 100 we add 2 zeros to the right.
To multiply by 200, 300, 400, we multiply by 2, 3, 4, and add two zeros.

$$16 \times 100 = 1\,600 \qquad 27 \times 200 = 5\,400 \qquad 19 \times 400 = 7\,600$$

A Now write down the answers to the following:

	(a)	(b)	(c)	(d)	(e)
1.	13×10	14×100	16×300	15×400	17×500
2.	29×10	23×400	24×200	12×300	9×600
3.	6×800	21×500	48×50	52×60	92×30

B Work these multiplication sums:

	(a)	(b)	(c)	(d)	(e)
1.	24×13	36×14	53×15	48×17	62×16
2.	53×24	65×24	72×28	46×53	57×48
3.	291×36	184×35	277×52	396×19	473×25
4.	126×15	235×18	342×23	403×36	320×50

Example $489 \div 21$

```
      23 r6  Answer
21)489    (a) How many 2's in 4? . . . . . 2
   42     (b) Multiply 21 by 2 . . . . . 42
   69     (c) Put 2 in answer  (d) Subtract
   63     (e) Take down next figure
    6     (f) Divide and continue as before.
```

C Now work the following:

	(a)	(b)
1.	$21\,)\,252$	$31\,)\,341$
2.	$21\,)\,6\,594$	$14\,)\,2\,968$
3.	$21\,)\,8\,841$	$31\,)\,3\,813$
4.	$21\,)\,7\,161$	$42\,)\,8\,869$
5.	$32\,)\,9\,961$	$43\,)\,9\,589$
6.	$42\,)\,5\,082$	$44\,)\,4\,930$

D

X	1	2	3	4	5	6	7	8	9
13	13	26	39	52	65	78	91	104	117
14	14	28	42	56	70	84	98	112	126
15	15	30	45	60	75	90	105	120	135
16	16	32	48	64	80	96	112	128	144
17	17	34	51	68	85	102			
18	18	36	54						
19	19	38							
20	20	40							
21	21	42							
22	22	44							
23	23	46							
24	24	48							
25	25	50							

Here is part of a table showing the numbers 13 to 25 multiplied by 1, 2, 3, ... 9. Study it and see how the numbers in each row and in each column increase each time. If you can see this, you will have found an easy way of making up a multiplication table by adding. No doubt you will see that the easiest way is to start at the top of each column and work downwards. Copy the table and complete it.

Use your table to give the answers to the following multiplication and division sums. You can see that:

16 × 4 = 64 and 102 ÷ 17 = 6

	(a)	(b)	(c)	(d)	(e)	(f)
1.	15 × 5	17 × 6	14 × 8	16 × 9	18 × 6	25 × 7
2.	24 × 9	23 × 7	6 × 18	7 × 19	8 × 22	25 × 17
3.	64 ÷ 4	85 ÷ 5	112 ÷ 8	144 ÷ 16	207 ÷ 9	176 ÷ 8
4.	68 ÷ 17	105 ÷ 15	153 ÷ 17	152 ÷ 19	176 ÷ 22	225 ÷ 25

Suppose we want to divide 120 by 16. If we look along the 16 row we find that the number *nearest to but less than* 120 is 112.

112 ÷ 16 = 7   So 120 ÷ 16 = 7, r 8.

Similarly   **100 ÷ 15 = 6, r 10.**

Find the answers:

	(a)	(b)	(c)	(d)	(e)	(f)
5.	100 ÷ 19	150 ÷ 18	106 ÷ 21	165 ÷ 23	102 ÷ 24	218 ÷ 25
6.	110 ÷ 17	85 ÷ 16	160 ÷ 19	108 ÷ 13	142 ÷ 22	100 ÷ 23

E Now work the following. Try to do them without using the table.
Do column (a) first, then column (b) and so on.

(a)	(b)	(c)	(d)	(e)	(f)
1. 21) 5 166	21) 168	32) 347	21) 2 226	21) 4 851	16) 336
2. 23) 3 933	31) 1 612	23) 705	21) 4 348	42) 9 716	17) 646
3. 22) 4 686	21) 1 365	21) 847	31) 3 255	13) 4 082	18) 756
4. 21) 2 562	32) 2 048	21) 1 365	31) 6 293	42) 2 712	19) 646
5. 31) 3 565	31) 3 751	32) 2 376	42) 8 672	14) 3 402	15) 3 465
6. 21) 6 531	44) 2 745	33) 1 995	33) 6 768	16) 3 696	26) 6 573
7. 41) 8 698	33) 1 095	41) 8 614	24) 4 912	23) 9 685	27) 3 949
8. 31) 3 813	21) 1 585	23) 5 080	22) 8 932	15) 3 215	45) 1 310

F In some of the following problems you divide, in others you multiply.
Think carefully before you start.

1. In a school there are 14 classes. Each class has 38 pupils. How many pupils are in the school?

2. A factory uses 250 litres of oil each week. How many litres in 26 weeks?

3. How many motor coaches would be required to take 896 factory workers on an outing to Blackpool, if each coach carries 32 people?

4. In a school there are 544 pupils. In each class there are 34 pupils. How many classes are there in the school?

5. In this book there are 96 pages. How many pages in 40 books?

6. A tobacconist has 1 160 cigars which he makes up into boxes of 20. How many boxes does he need?

7. A gross is 144 (12 dozen). How many books are there in 15 gross?

8. In a concert hall there are 28 rows of seats with 24 seats in each row. How many seats are there in the hall?

9. How many boxes will be needed to hold 360 eggs, if each box holds 24 eggs?

10. A small bag of coal weighs 14 kg. What is the weight of 16 bags?

11. 14 stone slabs weigh 182 kg.
    (a) What is the weight of 1 slab?
    (b) What is the weight of 24 slabs?

12. A man earns £18 a week. How much does he earn in a year?
    (1 year = 52 weeks.)

13. How many times is 21 contained in 399?

14. What is 25 times 89?

Time

A You should know that:

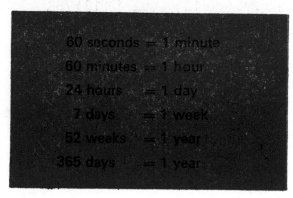

60 seconds	= 1 minute
60 minutes	= 1 hour
24 hours	= 1 day
7 days	= 1 week
52 weeks	= 1 year
365 days	= 1 year

1. How many sec in $\frac{1}{2}$ min, $\frac{1}{4}$ min, $1\frac{1}{2}$ min?

2. How many min in $\frac{1}{2}$ hr, $\frac{1}{4}$ hr, $\frac{3}{4}$ hr, $1\frac{1}{2}$ hr?

3. How many hours in 2 days?

4. How many days in 2 weeks, 3 weeks, 4 weeks?

5. How many weeks in 6 months?

6. Do you know this old rhyme? If not, learn it.

Thirty days has September,
April, June and November,
All the rest have thirty-one,
Except February alone,
Which has twenty-eight days clear,
And twenty-nine in each leap year.

Write in a column the twelve months of the year, and after each, write the number of days in the month.

7. When counting the number of days from one date to another, don't count the first date.

How many days are there from:

(a) 2nd June to 30th June
(b) 4th May to 30th May
(c) 4th May to 5th June
(d) 1st Oct to 31st Oct

(e) 9th June to 21st July
(f) 1st July to 5th August
(g) 3rd Aug to 30th Sept
(h) 1st Oct to 21st Nov?

B We have already learned that:

25 minutes past 10 in the morning is 10.25 a.m.;

a quarter to 10 at night is 9.45 p.m.

We always write the hour first, and after it the number of minutes past the hour.

14

1. Write these times in this way:

<table>
<tr><td colspan="2" align="center">Morning</td><td colspan="2" align="center">Afternoon and Evening</td></tr>
<tr><td>(a) half past 8</td><td>(d) a quarter past 9</td><td>(g) 10 min past 8</td><td>(j) a quarter to 6</td></tr>
<tr><td>(b) 25 min to 10</td><td>(e) 10 min to 11</td><td>(h) 5 min to 12</td><td>(k) half past 5</td></tr>
<tr><td>(c) 20 min past 7</td><td>(f) a quarter to 8</td><td>(i) 6 min to 10</td><td>(l) 20 min to 8</td></tr>
</table>

2.

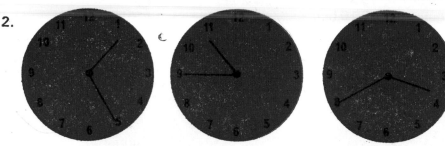

Morning Times   Afternoon Times

(a) Write the time on each of these clocks, using a.m. and p.m.
(b) Each of the first two clocks is 20 minutes slow.
Write the correct time.
(c) Each of the last two clocks is half-an-hour fast.
Write the correct time.

3. How many hours and minutes are there from:

<table>
<tr><td>(a) 9 a.m. to 10.30 a.m.</td><td>(d) 7.45 p.m. to 9 p.m.</td><td>(g) 10 a.m. to 12.30 p.m.</td></tr>
<tr><td>(b) 10 a.m. to 11.45 a.m.</td><td>(e) 6.30 p.m. to 10.45 p.m.</td><td>(h) 8.30 a.m. to 2.30 p.m.</td></tr>
<tr><td>(c) 8.30 a.m. to 12 noon</td><td>(f) 3.20 p.m. to 6 p.m.</td><td>(j) 8.45 p.m. to 10 p.m.?</td></tr>
</table>

C

Railway and Air Travel Time-tables do not use a.m. and p.m. times. Instead they use the 24-hour clock times.
On this clock the hours are numbered from each midnight to the next, from 0 to 24.
Times from 1 p.m. onwards are shown by adding 12 hours.
So 1 p.m. is 13 hours, 3 p.m. is 15 hours, and so on.

To avoid mistakes in time-tables all times are shown by 4 figures.

So 2 p.m. is written as 14.00 hours; 3.30 p.m. is 15.30 hours:
9.15 a.m. is 09.15 hours: 7.40 a.m. is 07.40 hours.

15

1. Write these times as 24-hour clock times:

2 p.m.	3.15 p.m.	4.40 p.m.	8.12 p.m.	5.20 p.m.	9.10 p.m.
1.50 p.m.	7.19 p.m.	8.50 a.m.	9.10 a.m.	6.5 a.m.	7.15 a.m.

2. Read these 24-hour clock times in the ordinary way, using a.m. and p.m.:

15.00 hours	14.00 hours	13.20 hours	15.25 hours	08.10 hours
21.00 hours	17.00 hours	18.10 hours	20.05 hours	06.20 hours

How many hours and minutes between 12.28 hours and 16.40 hours?

hr	min	
16	40	
12	28	
4	12	(Subtract)

How many hours and minutes between 13.40 hours and 18.30 hours?

hr	min	We cannot take 40 from 30 So add 60 min to min column and 1 hr to hr column
18	30	
13	40	
4	50	

3. Now find the number of hours and minutes from:

(a) 11.10 hours to 21.30 hours
(b) 12.15 hours to 20.45 hours
(c) 14.20 hours to 19.25 hours
(d) 15.25 hours to 20.50 hours
(e) 10.30 hours to 16.45 hours
(f) 13.05 hours to 18.20 hours

(g) 07.15 hours to 12.05 hours
(h) 06.45 hours to 09.00 hours
(i) 08.50 hours to 13.00 hours
(j) 16.40 hours to 19.50 hours
(k) 18.30 hours to 20.10 hours
(l) 15.15 hours to 18.05 hours

4. Here is a part of a railway time-table. It shows the times when four trains leave London and when they arrive in Glasgow.

(a) Find how long each train takes to travel from London to Glasgow.

(b) Which is the fastest train?

(c) Which is the slowest train?

(d) How much longer does this train take than the fastest train?

(e) Make another table showing these times as ordinary clock times, using a.m. and p.m.

London leave	Glasgow arrive
10.05	16.40
13.15	20.50
14.05	21.20
16.05	22.45

Money

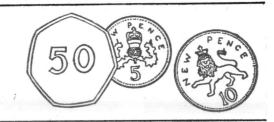

A You know that:
£1 = 100 new pence = 100p
£1·45 = £1 and 45p   (we say "one pound forty-five")
£2·80 = £2 and 80p   (two pounds eighty)
£2·08 = £2 and 8p   (two pounds eight)
£1·16½ = £1 and 16½p   (one pound sixteen and a half)

There are always two figures after the decimal point, since new pence (p) are hundredths of £1.
The **decimal point** separates the pound and the new pence.

1. Write the following, using the £ sign and the decimal point:

   (a) two pounds and sixty new pence.
   (b) four pounds and six new pence.
   (c) six pounds and 7p.
   (d) five pounds forty
   (e) five pounds four.
   (f) one pound nine.

   Amounts less than £1 can be written in two ways:

   80 new pence can be written: 80p or £0·80
   8 new pence can be written: 8p or £0·08

   The first way is much easier to write and is usually used on price labels in shops.

2. Write these using the £ sign and the decimal point:
   35p   40p   ·4p   9p   5p   1½p

3. Write these as p: (a) £0·75   (b) £0·50   (c) £0·07   (d) £0·02

4. Here is what 4 boys have in their money boxes.

	50p	10p	5p	2p	1p	½p
Jack	3	8	5	7	4	6
Bill	5	6	4	10	9	3
Ian	6	9	7	5	8	5
Jim	9	3	8	6	8	4

   (a) How much money has each boy?
   (b) How much has Jim more than Jack?
   (c) How much has Bill less than Ian?
   (d) How much more would Ian need to have as much as Jim?
   (e) If all the money was divided **equally** among the four boys, how much would each have?

17

B. Our money is a decimal coinage and so we add, subtract, multiply and divide as in decimals. Note where we put the £ sign in the examples below.

Add:	Subtract:	Multiply:	Divide:
£	£	£	£9·37
3·50	8·25	6·34	4) £37·48
1·65	2·90	×12	
2·48	———	———	
———	5·35	76·08	
7·63			

Now work the following. Remember there must always be two figures after the point in the answer.

1. (a) £1·25+£3·06+£2·80   (b) £0·42+£12·65+£2·09

2. (a) £8·63—£0·85   (b) £5·20—£2·34   (c) £7·12—£4·68

3. (a) £2·35×4   (b) £5·70×6   (c) £3·18×9   (d) £2·46×7

4. (a) £7·35÷3   (b) £5·32÷4   (c) £2·58÷6   (d) £1·05÷7

C 1. I had 45½p change from £1. How much did I spend?

2. Sandra wants £16·10 to buy a bicycle. She has already saved £12·15. How much more does she need?

3. Mother spent £1·65 at the grocer's and 78p at the butcher's.

   (a) How much money did she spend?
   (b) How much had she left from £5?

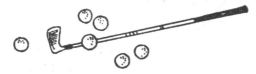

4. Dad bought a golf club for £4·75 and six golf balls for £1·74.

   (a) How much did he spend?
   (b) He paid with two £5 notes. How much change did he get?
   (c) What is the cost of a golf ball?

5. I require £1·12 more to have £5. How much have I?

6. Dad bought a pair of shoes for £4·25, a shirt for £2·55 and a tie for 86p.

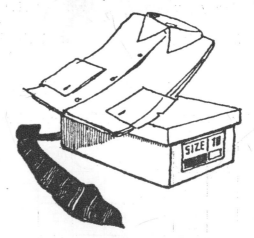

   (a) How much did he spend?
   (b) How much change from two £5 notes?

1. Find the total cost of:

(a) 2 boxes of chocolates
3 tins of biscuits
½ kg of cheese
2 packets of cornflakes
2 tins of tomato soup

(b) 2 tins of biscuits
3 jars of honey
3 tins of tomato soup
3 packets of cornflakes
¼ kg of cheese

(c) 5 tins of biscuits
4 jars of honey
4 packets of cornflakes
5 tins of tomato soup
3 tubes of Smarties.

(d) 1½ kg of cheese
2 jars of honey
4 tins of biscuits
4 tins of tomato soup
5 tubes of Smarties.

2. A merchant bought 70m of cloth at 95p per metre and 12m at £1·35 per metre. How much less than £100 did this cost?

3. Jim bought a bicycle for £14·50 and sold it for £17·25. How much profit did he make?

4. If a dozen of these Maths books cost £5·76, what would I pay for 1 book?

5. A sports club bought 3 hockey sticks at £2·39 each, 4 tennis rackets at £3·95 each, a dozen tennis balls at 23p each, and 2 footballs at £2·98 each. What was the total cost?

6.

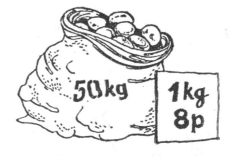

I bought 3½ kg of potatoes.
(a) How much had I to pay?
(b) How much change did I get from £1?
(c) For how much was the whole bag sold?

Decimals

A We have already learned another way—the decimal way—of writing tenths:

$\frac{4}{10} = 0.4$ $\frac{5}{10} = 0.5$ $3\frac{7}{10} = 3.7$, and so on.

1 Here are some picture numbers. Write the numbers in figures, using the decimal point.

H	T	U • tenths

H	T	U • tenths

H	T	U • tenths

H	T	U • tenths

2 Draw picture numbers of your own to show:

   (a) 402·4   (b) 143·5   (c) 76·8   (d) 10·2   (e) 260·6

3

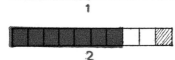
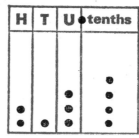
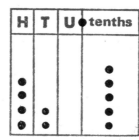
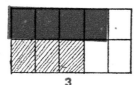
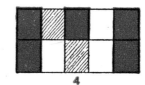
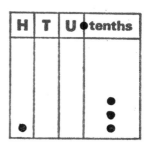

  (1) How many equal divisions are there in each figure?

  (2) What part of each figure is (a) coloured (b) shaded (c) white?
     Write this in two ways, like this: Figure 1: coloured $\frac{5}{10} = 0.5$
                                   shaded $\frac{3}{10} = 0.3$
                                     white $\frac{2}{10} = 0.2$

4 Write in decimal form: $\frac{3}{10}$ $\frac{5}{10}$ $\frac{7}{10}$ $\frac{9}{10}$ $\frac{8}{10}$ $\frac{1}{10}$ $\frac{4}{10}$ $\frac{2}{10}$

5 We know that the decimal point separates whole numbers from the tenths.

  2·5 means 2 wholes and 5 tenths   3·8 means 3 wholes and 8 tenths
  1·6 means 1 whole and 6 tenths   0·9 means no wholes and 9 tenths

  Write these as decimal fractions:

  (a) 4 wholes and 8 tenths   (b) 4 wholes and 2 tenths   (c) 1 whole and 5 tenths
  (d) 6 „   „ 9 „   (e) 7 „   „ 6 „   (f) no „   „ 7 „
  (g) 5 „   „ 7 „   (h) 8 „   „ 8 „   (i) no „   „ 4 „

6 Write these numbers in order of size, putting the smallest first.

    (a) 3·0   30   0·3   33   (c) 0·8   8·0   80

    (b) 44   4·4   4·0   0·4   (d) 5·0   50   0·5

7 Change these decimals to ordinary fractions, giving each fraction in its lowest terms. An example is done for you.

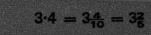

$$3·4 = 3\tfrac{4}{10} = 3\tfrac{2}{5}$$

    0·4   0·6   0·8   0·2   9·5   7·9   3·4   6·3

    3·6   4·2   5·5   6·4   2·7   2·8   5·1   8·6

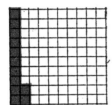

This figure is divided into 100 small squares. You can see that 12 out of the 100 squares are coloured.

$$\tfrac{12}{100} = \tfrac{1}{10} + \tfrac{2}{100} = ·12$$

So in decimals the first figure after the point stands for tenths, the second figure after the point for hundredths.

$$3·65 = 3 \text{ wholes} + 6 \text{ tenths} + 5 \text{ hundredths} = 3\tfrac{65}{100} = 3\tfrac{13}{20}$$

8 Write in this way, giving the fraction in its simplest form:

    2·45   3·15   5·75   3·25   6·05   4·95

9 Write as decimals:

    $1\tfrac{13}{100}$ $2\tfrac{25}{100}$ $4\tfrac{43}{100}$ $\tfrac{24}{100}$ $\tfrac{5}{100}$

    Note: When we have no whole number, as in the last two above, it is a good idea to show this by a zero. So $\tfrac{75}{100} = 0·75$

B Adding and subtracting decimals

When adding or subtracting decimals, put the points under each other, making sure that the point in the answer is under the other points.

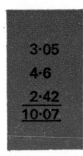

    3·05
    4·6
    2·42
    10·07

1 Add:

    (a) 2·63   (b) 4·75   (c) 17·37

         1·08   2·62   8·06

         4·75   3·48   4·14

    (d) 3·84 + 2·5 + 0·05

    (e) 16·2 + 5·85 + 9·75

    (f) 7·02 + 8·25 + 4·8

    (g) 4·75 + 3·49 + 10·05

    (h) 9·25 + 6·75 + 12·05

2 Subtract:
   (a) 12·85 — 6·29
   (b) 10·25 — 8·48
   (c) 9·40 — 3·65
   (d) 25·05 — 8·76
   (e) 9·2 — 3·75
   (f) 8·5 — 6·38
   (g) 30·06 — 12·84
   (h) 16·5 — 9·87
   (i) 6·0 — 2·25

3 In a motor car there is a speedometer to show the speed at which the car is travelling. Beside it there is another instrument which records the number of km the car has travelled. It shows this in whole kilometres and tenths of a km. The tenths are usually shown in red. As each tenth of a km is passed the reading changes.

| 0 | 0 | 6 | 5 | 2 | 8 |

This reading shows that the car has travelled 652·8 km.

Write down these distance recorder readings:

| 0 | 0 | 7 | 2 | 3 | **5** |

(a)

| 0 | 6 | 2 | 5 | 3 | **7** |

(b)

| 0 | 7 | 2 | 9 | 8 | **2** |

(c)

| 1 | 7 | 4 | 8 | 6 | **4** |

(d)

Look at the readings below. They are in pairs. In each case the first reading gives the number of km shown on the distance recorder at the beginning of a journey. The second reading shows the number of km on the distance recorder at the end of the journey. Find the length of each journey.

| 0 | 0 | 5 | 4 | 2 | 2 |
| 0 | 0 | 6 | 6 | 0 | 7 |

(e)

| 0 | 4 | 3 | 1 | 7 | **5** |
| 0 | 4 | 3 | 9 | 2 | **3** |

(f)

| 0 | 8 | 4 | 2 | 0 | 6 |
| 0 | 9 | 5 | 4 | 7 | 1 |

(g)

| 1 | 6 | 4 | 8 | 9 | **8** |
| 1 | 6 | 6 | 2 | 3 | **2** |

(h)

C Multiplication and Division by a whole number

Multiply as with whole numbers, but make sure that you put a point in the answer directly under the point in the number being multiplied.

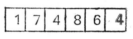

$$\begin{array}{r} 6·74 \\ \times 6 \\ \hline 40·44 \end{array}$$

Multiply:
1 (a) 4·25
   ×5
   (b) 5·36
   ×4
   (c) 6·94
   ×6
   (d) 3·75
   ×5
   (e) 7·38
   ×3
   (f) 6·03
   ×9

Divide as with whole numbers, but make sure that the point in the answer is directly above the point in the number being divided.

$$6\overline{)32·58} \quad 5·43$$

2 (a) 4)13·04
   (b) 6)28·38
   (c) 8)42·72
   (d) 3)25·71
   (e) 21)95·55

   (f) 3)28·71
   (g) 5)42·15
   (h) 6)42·18
   (i) 5)41·35
   (j) 32)77·76

D Multiplying and Dividing by 10 and 100

Mark two cardboard or paper strips
as shown.

(a) Place a strip A above strip B
   to show 2·64.
   To multiply 2·64 by 10, slide
   B one box to the left.
   So 2·64 × 10 = 26·4.
   To multiply 2·64 by 100, slide B
   two boxes to the left.
   So 2·64 × 100 = 264.

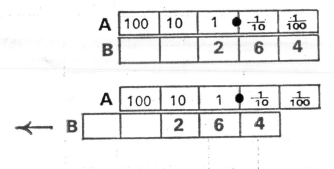

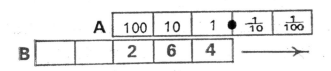

(b) Here 264 is shown.

   To divide 264 by 10, slide B one
   box to the right.
   So 264 ÷ 10 = 26·4
   To divide 264 by 100, slide B two
   boxes to the right.
   So 264 ÷ 100 = 2·64

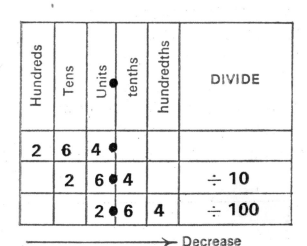

(c) Here is what happens.

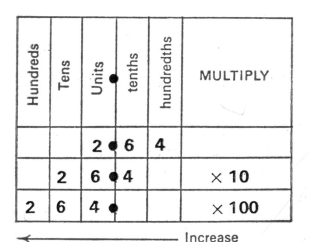

Hundreds	Tens	Units	tenths	hundredths	MULTIPLY
		2•6	4		
	2	6•4			× 10
2	6	4•			× 100

←———————— Increase

Hundreds	Tens	Units	tenths	hundredths	DIVIDE
2	6	4•			
	2	6•4			÷ 10
		2•6	4		÷ 100

Decrease ———————→

Write the answers to the following. Use your strips if you like.

	(a)	(b)	(c)	(d)	(e)
1	2·64 × 10	3·58 × 10	6·75 × 10	4·23 × 10	7·86 × 10
2	2·64 × 100	3·58 × 100	6·75 × 100	4·23 × 100	7·86 × 100
3	532 ÷ 10	235 ÷ 10	617 ÷ 10	901 ÷ 10	648 ÷ 10
4	532 ÷ 100	235 ÷ 100	617 ÷ 100	901 ÷ 100	648 ÷ 100

23

Fractions

	1		2	Halves
1	2	3	4	Quarters
1 2 3	4 5	6 7 8		Eighths

A

(a) A number line from 0 to 1 divided into halves (top: 0, ½, 1) and quarters (bottom: 0, ¼, 2/4, ¾, 4/4).

(b) A number line from 0 to 1 divided into thirds (top: 0, ⅓, ⅔, 1) and sixths (bottom: 0, 1/6, 2/6, 3/6, 4/6, 5/6, 6/6).

(c) A number line from 0 to 1 divided into fifths (top: 0, 1/5, 2/5, 3/5, 4/5, 1) and tenths (bottom: 0, 1/10, 2/10, 3/10, 4/10, 5/10, 6/10, 7/10, 8/10, 9/10, 10/10).

In the "number lines" above the top line is divided into:

(a) 2 equal parts   (b) 3 equal parts   (c) 5 equal parts

The bottom lines have the same length but are divided into quarters, sixths and tenths.

1. Write $\frac{1}{2}$ in quarters, sixths and tenths.
2. Write down 2 other ways of writing $\frac{1}{3}$ and $\frac{2}{3}$.
3. Write $\frac{1}{5}$, $\frac{2}{5}$, $\frac{3}{5}$, $\frac{4}{5}$ in tenths.
4. Write 1 whole in 3 other ways.
5. (a) How many quarters in $\frac{1}{2}$, $\frac{3}{4}$?   (b) How many sixths in $\frac{1}{3}$, $\frac{2}{3}$, 1 whole?
   (c) How many tenths in $\frac{1}{5}$, $\frac{3}{5}$, $\frac{4}{5}$, 1 whole?
   (d) From the "number lines" above, what is: $\frac{1}{2}$ of $\frac{1}{2}$, $\frac{1}{2}$ of $\frac{1}{3}$, $\frac{1}{2}$ of $\frac{2}{3}$, $\frac{1}{2}$ of $\frac{4}{5}$?
   (e) Can you find a quicker way of answering the questions in (d) without a drawing?

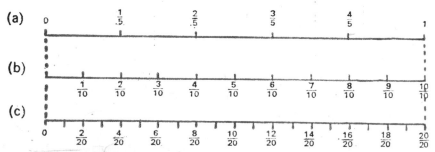

(a) A number line from 0 to 1 divided into fifths (0, 1/5, 2/5, 3/5, 4/5, 1).

(b) A number line from 0 to 1 divided into tenths (1/10, 2/10, 3/10, 4/10, 5/10, 6/10, 7/10, 8/10, 9/10, 10/10).

(c) A number line from 0 to 1 divided into twentieths (0, 2/20, 4/20, 6/20, 8/20, 10/20, 12/20, 14/20, 16/20, 18/20, 20/20).

B 1. (a) Into how many parts is each of the 3 lines divided?

(b) What is the length (in cm) of each part of the 3 lines?

(c) Write down as many equivalent (equal) fractions as you can.
You can see from the number line that $\frac{2}{5} = \frac{4}{10} = \frac{8}{20}$.

24

2. (a) How many fifths in: $\frac{4}{10}$ $\frac{6}{10}$ $\frac{8}{10}$ $\frac{4}{20}$ $\frac{12}{20}$ $\frac{16}{20}$?

    (b) How many tenths in: $\frac{1}{5}$ $\frac{2}{5}$ $\frac{4}{5}$ $\frac{4}{20}$ $\frac{8}{20}$ $\frac{12}{20}$?

    (c) How many twentieths in: $\frac{1}{5}$ $\frac{3}{5}$ $\frac{4}{5}$ $\frac{1}{10}$ $\frac{3}{10}$ $\frac{7}{10}$?

    (d) A boy got 4 marks out of a total of 5 marks.

       (1) What fraction of the total did he score?

       (2) What would he have scored out of totals of 10 marks, 20 marks, 50 marks?

C We can use our "number lines" to add and subtract fractions.
Here are 2 parts of the number lines shown in B on the opposite page.

Fig. (1)   **Fig. (2)**

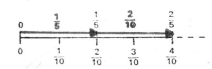   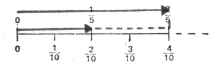

Fig. 1 shows: $\frac{1}{5} + \frac{2}{10} = \frac{4}{10} = \frac{2}{5}$ Fig 2 shows: $\frac{4}{10} - \frac{1}{5} = \frac{4}{10} - \frac{2}{10} = \frac{2}{10} = \frac{1}{5}$

Now use the number lines you have drawn to find:

	(a)	(b)	(c)	(d)	(e)
1.	$\frac{3}{10} + \frac{4}{10}$	$\frac{1}{10} + \frac{8}{10}$	$\frac{3}{10} + \frac{2}{10}$	$\frac{1}{10} + \frac{9}{10}$	$\frac{1}{5} + \frac{2}{5}$
2.	$\frac{2}{5} + \frac{3}{5}$	$\frac{6}{10} + \frac{2}{5}$	$\frac{3}{5} + \frac{2}{10}$	$\frac{3}{10} + \frac{4}{20}$	$\frac{4}{10} + \frac{7}{20}$
3.	$\frac{6}{10} - \frac{2}{10}$	$1 - \frac{7}{10}$	$\frac{4}{10} - \frac{1}{5}$	$\frac{9}{10} - \frac{4}{5}$	$\frac{4}{5} - \frac{3}{10}$
4.	$\frac{6}{10} - \frac{7}{20}$	$\frac{9}{10} - \frac{14}{20}$	$\frac{4}{5} - \frac{7}{20}$	$\frac{3}{5} - \frac{8}{20}$	$1 - \frac{17}{20}$

D We have found that: $\frac{1}{2} = \frac{2}{4} = \frac{3}{6} = \frac{5}{10} = \frac{10}{20}$
You can see that each of these is the same if we multiply, or divide, the numerator and denominator by the same number (2, 3, 4, 5 and so on).

1. Fill in the missing number in each of these equal fractions:

    (a) $\frac{1}{3} = \frac{2}{} = \frac{}{9} = \frac{4}{} = \frac{}{15}$ (b) $\frac{}{5} = \frac{2}{10} = \frac{4}{} = \frac{}{30} = \frac{10}{}$

2. A cake was cut into several equal slices. Jean ate half the cake. If the cake was cut into 10 slices, then Jean had 5 slices.
How many slices would she have eaten, if the cake was divided into: 4 slices, 6 slices, 8 slices, 12 slices, 14 slices?

3. An hour is divided into 60 minutes. So 1 minute $= \frac{1}{60}$ of an hour.

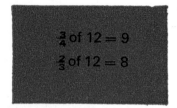

$40 \text{ min} = \frac{40}{60}$ of an hour;

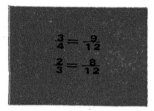

$\frac{40}{60} = \frac{20}{30} = \frac{2}{3}$;

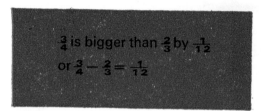

$40 \text{ min} = \frac{2}{3}$ of an hour.

We say that $\frac{2}{3}$ is the simplest form of the fraction $\frac{40}{60}$.

What fraction of an hour (in the simplest form) is 2 min, 5 min, 20 min, 45 min?

4. Would you rather have $\frac{2}{3}$ of £12 or $\frac{3}{4}$ of £12?

You would want to find which is bigger: $\frac{2}{3}$ or $\frac{3}{4}$.

To find this out, we want something that breaks (or divides) easily into thirds and quarters, like a dozen.

$\frac{3}{4}$ of $12 = 9$

$\frac{2}{3}$ of $12 = 8$

$\frac{3}{4} = \frac{9}{12}$

$\frac{2}{3} = \frac{8}{12}$

$\frac{3}{4}$ is bigger than $\frac{2}{3}$ by $\frac{1}{12}$

or $\frac{3}{4} - \frac{2}{3} = \frac{1}{12}$

You can see this on the number line divided into 12 equal parts.

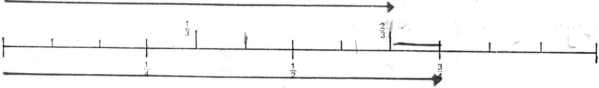

Which is bigger and by how much:

(a) $\frac{2}{3}$ or $\frac{5}{12}$ (b) $\frac{1}{2}$ or $\frac{7}{12}$ (c) $\frac{3}{4}$ or $\frac{11}{12}$ (d) $\frac{5}{12}$ or $\frac{1}{3}$ (e) $\frac{4}{6}$ or $\frac{5}{12}$?

E 1. A boy lost $\frac{1}{5}$ and then $\frac{3}{10}$ of his marbles. What fraction had he left?

2. Ann spent $\frac{3}{8}$ of her money in one shop and $\frac{1}{4}$ in another.

(a) What fraction of her money had she left?

(b) If she had 48p, what did she spend in each shop, and how much had she left?

3. Tom travelled $\frac{5}{12}$ of his journey by train, $\frac{1}{4}$ by steamer, and the rest by bus. If he travelled 84 kilometres altogether, how far did he go by bus?

4. $\frac{2}{3}$ of a class have brown hair, $\frac{1}{4}$ have fair hair and the rest black hair. What fraction of the class has black hair?

5. A sum of money was divided among 3 boys. Tom got $\frac{5}{12}$ and Jack got $\frac{1}{3}$.

(a) What fraction did Dick get?

(b) Who got the most money?

6. At a sale $\frac{3}{8}$ of the goods were sold one day and $\frac{1}{2}$ the next day. What fraction of the goods was unsold?

26

F Multiplying a fraction by a whole number

3 apples $\times 5 = 15$ apples and 3 fifths $\times 5 = 15$ fifths

3 fifths $\times 5 = 15$ may be written as $\frac{3}{5} \times 5 = \frac{15}{5}$

From this you can see that **to multiply a fraction by a whole number we multiply the numerator by that number.**

Here we see $\frac{3}{5} \times 5$ on the number line divided into 15 equal parts.

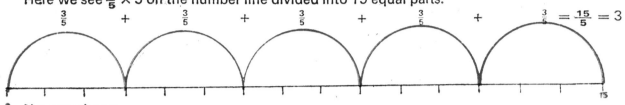

$$\frac{3}{5} + \frac{3}{5} + \frac{3}{5} + \frac{3}{5} + \frac{3}{5} = \frac{15}{5} = 3$$

Now try these:

(a)	(b)	(c)	(d)	(e)	(f)
1. $\frac{1}{2} \times 6$	$\frac{1}{4} \times 8$	$\frac{1}{5} \times 10$	$\frac{1}{6} \times 12$	$\frac{1}{10} \times 20$	$\frac{1}{20} \times 60$
2. $\frac{3}{4} \times 8$	$\frac{2}{5} \times 20$	$\frac{3}{5} \times 40$	$\frac{5}{6} \times 18$	$\frac{3}{10} \times 20$	$\frac{3}{20} \times 40$

> $\frac{1}{2} \times 6$ is the same as $\frac{1}{2}$ of 6

> $\frac{5}{6} \times 18$ is the same as $\frac{5}{6}$ of 18

Find:

(a)	(b)	(c)	(d)	(e)
3. $\frac{1}{2}$ of £30	$\frac{1}{4}$ of £20	$\frac{1}{5}$ of 40 cm	$\frac{1}{6}$ of 12 kg	$\frac{1}{10}$ of 30 litres
4. $\frac{3}{4}$ of £24	$\frac{2}{3}$ of 30 m	$\frac{4}{5}$ of 30 kg	$\frac{5}{6}$ of 24 km	$\frac{3}{10}$ of 20 litres

G Dividing a fraction by a whole number

From the number line: $\frac{1}{4} \div 2 = \frac{1}{8}$ $\qquad \frac{1}{8} \div 2 = \frac{1}{16}$ $\qquad \frac{3}{4} \div 2 = \frac{6}{8} \div 2 = \frac{3}{8}$

So to divide a fraction by a whole number, multiply the denominator by that number.

Now try these:

(a)	(b)	(c)	(d)	(e)
1. $\frac{1}{2} \div 3$	$\frac{1}{4} \div 2$	$\frac{2}{3} \div 3$	$\frac{3}{4} \div 6$	$\frac{4}{5} \div 2$
2. $\frac{1}{4} \div 3$	$\frac{3}{5} \div 6$	$\frac{2}{3} \div 4$	$\frac{7}{8} \div 2$	$\frac{2}{5} \div 4$

H Multiplying by a fraction

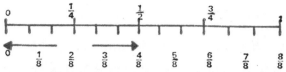

From the number line you can see that

$\frac{3}{4}$ covers 9 small divisions, and $\frac{2}{3}$ of 9 = 6 small divisions = $\frac{1}{2}$ of the whole line.

So $\frac{2}{3}$ of $\frac{3}{4} = \frac{1}{2}$ and $\frac{2}{3} \times \frac{3}{4} = \frac{2 \times 3}{3 \times 4} = \frac{6}{12} = \frac{1}{2}$

Now try these:

	(a)	(b)	(c)	(d)	(e)
1.	$\frac{1}{2} \times \frac{1}{2}$	$\frac{1}{4} \times \frac{1}{3}$	$\frac{1}{2} \times \frac{1}{3}$	$\frac{3}{4} \times \frac{1}{2}$	$\frac{1}{2} \times \frac{1}{4}$
2.	$\frac{2}{3} \times \frac{3}{5}$	$\frac{3}{4} \times \frac{2}{5}$	$\frac{1}{3}$ of $\frac{4}{5}$	$\frac{2}{3}$ of $\frac{3}{10}$	$\frac{3}{5}$ of $\frac{5}{6}$

I Dividing by a fraction

If 6 sweets are shared equally between 2 children, each gets 3 sweets ($6 \div 2 = 3$)

So $6 \div 2$ means "how many 2's are there in 6"?

In the same way $6 \div \frac{1}{2}$ means "how many halves in 6?"

From the number line you can see that there are 12 halves in 6 wholes.

So $6 \div \frac{1}{2} = 12$ and $6 \times 2 = 12$ (multiply by the fraction "upside down").

1. Work out in this way:

(a) $6 \div \frac{1}{3}$ (b) $8 \div \frac{1}{2}$ (c) $9 \div \frac{1}{3}$ (d) $10 \div \frac{1}{5}$ (e) $12 \div \frac{1}{2}$

(f) $12 \div \frac{1}{3}$ (g) $8 \div \frac{1}{4}$ (h) $20 \div \frac{1}{5}$ (i) $16 \div \frac{1}{2}$ (j) $10 \div \frac{1}{10}$

2. (a) A 6 kg bag of tea is divided into $\frac{1}{2}$ kg packets. How many $\frac{1}{2}$ kg packets are there?

(b) How many $\frac{1}{4}$ litre tumblers can be filled from a 5-litre can of lemonade?

(c) How many $\frac{1}{2}$p in: 10p, 20p, 50p, 80p?

(d) How many $\frac{1}{3}$ metres in: 6m, 10m, 5m?

(e) 20 bars of chocolate are shared equally among some boys. Each boy gets half a bar. How many boys are there?

(f) A 10 metre length of paper is divided into strips, each $\frac{1}{10}$ of a metre. How many strips are there?

From the answers to the questions above, it is clear that **to divide by a fraction, we turn the fraction "upside down" and then multiply.**

So $6 \div \frac{1}{3} = 6 \times \frac{3}{1} = 18$ and $\frac{1}{2} \div \frac{1}{4} = \frac{1}{2} \times \frac{4}{1} = \frac{4}{2} = 2$

J Now try these:

1. (a) $4 \div \frac{1}{3}$ (b) $\frac{1}{4} \div \frac{1}{2}$ (c) $\frac{1}{2} \div \frac{1}{4}$ (d) $\frac{1}{3} \div \frac{2}{3}$ (e) $\frac{1}{4} \div \frac{3}{8}$

(f) $\frac{1}{3} \div \frac{1}{2}$ (g) $\frac{3}{4} \div \frac{1}{2}$ (h) $\frac{3}{5} \div \frac{3}{10}$ (i) $\frac{9}{10} \div \frac{3}{5}$ (j) $\frac{2}{3} \div \frac{2}{5}$

Length

We already know that we measure length in METRES.

A metre is quite a large measure as you will see if you have a metre stick or a metre tape.

We use metres to measure the length of a garden path, the width of a room, the length and breadth of a field, the length of a race and so on.

We also measure in CENTIMETRES.

We would use centimetres to measure the length of a pencil, the size of a page, the width of a plank of wood, and so on.

> **1 metre (m) = 100 centimetres (cm)**
>
> **1 centimetre = $\frac{1}{100}$ metre = 0·01 metre**

1. How many cm are in: 2 m   3 m $1\frac{1}{2}$ m $2\frac{1}{2}$ m   5 m?
2. Write as m and cm: 145 cm   232 cm   565 cm   470 cm   618 cm.
3. Which is the greater and by how many cm: (a) 1 m or 75 cm   (b) 4·5 m or 420 cm?
4. Change to cm: (a) 1 m 35 cm   (b) 4 m 45 cm   (c) 2 m 5 cm   (d) 3 m 9 cm
5. Which is larger, and by how much, 725 cm or 7·5 m?

> Since a centimetre is a hundredth of a metre we can write:
>
> 425 cm as 4·25 m,   378 cm as 3·78 m,   and 106 cm as 1·06 m
>
> Note that the decimal point separates the metres from the centimetres.

6. Complete the following:
   - (a) 146 cm = 1 m 46 cm = 1·46 m
   - (b) 285 cm =
   - (c) 412 cm =
   - (d) 106 cm =
   - (e) 309 cm =

7. Complete the following:
   - (a) 2·35 m = 2 m 35 cm = 235 cm
   - (b) 4·16 m =
   - (c) 3·75 m =
   - (d) 1·03 m =
   - (e) 4·08 m =

B 1. Two planks of wood are laid end to end. One plank is 2 m 35 cm long and the other is 1 m 78 cm. What is their total length?

2. Three sticks each measuring 75 centimetres are placed end to end in a straight line. What is their total length?

3. A rope is 1·35 m long. If 85 cm is cut off, how much will be left?

4. Don is 40 cm taller than Ian who is 1·12m tall. How tall is Don?

5. Jack is 1 m 58 cm tall. Tim is 62 cm smaller. How tall is Tim?

6. If a rope 3 m 95 cm long is joined to another rope 2 m 47 cm long, what will be the total length?

7 4 parcels of equal size were tied in the same way. Each parcel needed 75 cm of string. How much string was used altogether?

8. A ball of string containing 30 metres of string is cut into 6 equal lengths. How long is each length in cm?

C 1. Estimate the length in cm of the following articles. Now check with your ruler to see if your estimates were good ones:

> your pencil
> a pen
> a chalk
> a knife
> a nail
> a brush
> this book (also its width)
> your exercise book (also its width)

2. Take a good look at the length of a metre stick. Now try to estimate the measurements of the following objects to the nearest $\frac{1}{2}$ metre:

> The blackboard (length and height)
> The door (length and height)
> The floor (length and breadth)

Check with your metre stick or tape to see how good your estimates were.

3. Guess the height of one of your classmates. Now ask him (or her) to stand upright against the wall. Hold a ruler or a book just touching the top of his head. Mark this height and then measure with a measuring tape. Do the same with two other classmates.

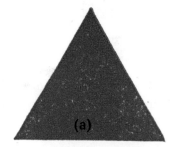
(a)

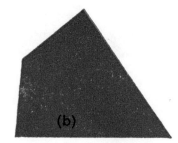
(b)

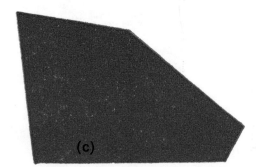
(c)

Measure the length of each side of the shapes above and then find the distance all round the shape. The length all round a shape is called the **perimeter.**

D In Book 2 we measured lines in **cm** and $\frac{1}{2}$ **cm**. On some rulers you will find between each of the **cm** marks a number of little marks like this:

cm   1   2   3   4   5

These small divisions are called MILLIMETRES.

Look at your ruler. Does it have millimetres (mm) marked on it?

If it does not, then look at the drawing above.

How many **mm** spaces are there in each cm?

You will see there are 10.

So we can now extend our table of length to read:

> 10 millimetres (mm) = 1 centimetre (cm)
>
> 100 centimetres (cm) = 1 metre (m)
>
> 1 000 millimetres = 1 metre

1. If your ruler has millimetres on it measure the lines below. Millimetres are so small that you may find it difficult to read them, but do your best. If your measurement is a millimetre more or less than it should be, don't worry. An approximate (near) measurement will be good enough. The first one is done for you.

(a) length = 5 cm 2 mm = 5·2 cm

(c)

(d)

2. Draw as near as you can lines of: 4·5 cm   5·4 cm   6·8 cm   3·7 cm

E Do you remember the name of the unit we use for measuring long distances such as the distances between towns?

It is the KILOMETRE which is equal to 1 000 METRES.

1. Write these lengths as km and m. The first one is done for you.

(a) 1 245 m = 1 000 m + 245 m = 1 km 245 m.

(b) 3 763 m   (c) 2 534 m   (d) 4 376 m   (e) 5 892 m   (f) 7 025 m

2. Write these lengths in **metres**:

(a) 4 km 125 m   (b) 3 km 750 m   (c) 3 km 926 m   (d) 6 km 897 m

Weight

A The unit of weight is the GRAMME (for short, g).
It is a very, very small weight. A fly would weigh just about a gramme.
A bigger weight we often use is the KILOGRAMME (kg).

1 KILOGRAMME = 1 000 GRAMMES

Sets of weights are often made up of:

1g   5g   10g   20g   50g   100g   500g   1000g
(1 kg)

1. Make up a table like this one:

Less than 10 g	Less than 50 g	Less than 100 g	Less than 500 g	Less than 1 kg	More than 1 kg
Drawing pin	Rubber		Milk bottle		

Now weigh some of the things in the classroom and put the names in the proper places in the table. Write the actual weights if you like.
Can you find many things less than 10 g?

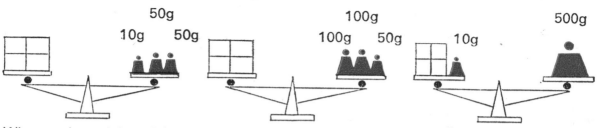

3. What are the weights of these parcels?

4. (a) Which two weights in the set of weights above would you use to weigh:

   110 g   25 g   150 g   520 g   1 kg 20 g $1\frac{1}{2}$ kg?

   (b) Which three weights to weigh:
   250 g   115 g   75 g   80 g   650 g   1 kg 550 g   1 kg 21 g?

32

5. What weights from the set shown would you use to balance each of these?

| 1 kilogramme = 1 000 grammes |
| So 1 kg 200 g = 1 200 g |
| and 2 kg 75 g = 2 075 g |

1. Write as grammes:

(a) 1 kg 325 g

(b) 2 kg 450 g

(c) 3 kg 86 g

(d) 4 kg 5 g

| 1 000 g = 1 kg |
| So 1 480 g = 1 kg 480 g |
| and 2 055 g = 2 kg 55 g |

2. Write as kg and g:

(a) 2 175 g

(b) 3 672 g

(c) 1 078 g

(d) 4 572 g

(e) 5 026 g

(f) 6 009 g

3. A bag holds 10 kg of sugar. How many packets, each weighing 500 g, can be filled from it?

4. What fraction of 1 kg is:

(a) 500 g

(b) 250 g

(c) 750 g

(d) 100 g

(e) 200 g

(f) 800 g?

5. Tom bought 500 g of butter, 2 tins of sardines each weighing 250 g, 2·5 kg of potatoes and 2·5 kg of apples. The shop assistant gave him a cardboard box which weighed 700 g to carry them home. What weight did he have to carry altogether?

C **1.** Miss Brown was going to teach in Australia for a year. The travel agency told her she could take only 66 kg of luggage in the aeroplane. When she packed her cases she found that one weighed 27 kg 300 g, another weighed 28 kg 730 g, and the smallest one weighed 10 kg 450 g. Did she have to unpack any of her cases?

2. Before she left Miss Brown gave each of the 32 children in her class a bag of toffees. Each bag weighed 250 g. What was the total weight of toffees she had to buy?

3. A baby should double its weight in 6 months. Linda weighed 2 kg 800 g when she was born. After 6 months she weighed 6 kg 100 g.

(a) Did she double her weight?

(b) Did she weigh more or less, and by how much?

4. Joe is the heaviest boy in the class. He weighs 45 kg. Sam is the next heaviest. He weighs only 350 g less than Joe. What does Sam weigh?

5. A box full of prunes weighed 18 kg 100 g. The empty box weighed 1 kg 150 g. What was the weight of the prunes?

6. Find the total cost of:

(a) 500 g at 72p per kg;

(b) 250 g at 60p per kg;

(c) 2 kg 750 g at 80p per kg.

Roundabout

We can use **round** numbers like 10 and 20, or 100 and 200 and so on, to give an **approximate** or **near** answer. If we want a near answer to a sum like 197 + 52, the answer is about 200 + 50, or 250.

1. Find approximate answers to:

   (a) 196 + 49   (b) 203 + 298   (c) 443 − 102   (d) 303 − 97
   (e) 203 × 12   (f) 243 ÷ 61   (g) 997 × 9   (h) 608 ÷ 29

   Look at this number:

   ## 873

   It lies between 870 and 880. It is nearer 870.
   So, to the nearest 10, we can say it is about 870.
   It lies between 800 and 900. It is nearer 900.
   So, to the nearest 100, we can say it is about 900.

2. (a) Write to the nearest 10: 27,   32,   88,   114,   398,   421,
   (b) Write to the nearest 100: 115,   269,   482,   968,   326,   731.

3.

Example 1:
$18\frac{1}{2}$ p is nearly 20 p
So $18\frac{1}{2}$ p × 4 is nearly 20 p × 4, or 80 p

Example 2:
1 kg 875 g is nearly 2 kg
So 1 kg 875 g × 9 is about 2 kg × 9, or 18 kg

Find in this way approximate (near) answers to:

(a) 98p × 9   (b) £1·89 × 6   (c) £2·97 × 8   (d) £4·88 × 12

(e) $29\frac{1}{2}$ kg × 8   (f) 3 kg 920 g × 12   (g) 2 875 cm × 7   (h) 5·026 kg × 5

(i) £9·05 ÷ 3   (j) 9 kg 896 g ÷ 5   (k) 412 m × 9   (l) 987 g ÷ 20

(m) About how much would I pay
    for 4 toys at $24\frac{1}{2}$ p each?

(n) A shop sold 25 metres of cloth
    at £1·92 per metre. About how much
    was paid for the cloth?

(o) A train travels at a speed of 80 km
    per hour. About how far does it
    travel in 2 hours 50 minutes?

(p) About how much would I pay for 6·8
    metres of carpet at £4·05 per metre?

Angles

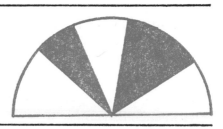

A We have already made a right angle from paper. We know that an angle smaller than a right angle is called an acute (sharp) angle, and an angle bigger than a right angle is called an obtuse (blunt) angle.

How do we measure the size of an angle? First of all we must know that an angle is just an amount of turning. We keep turning things every day. We turn a key to lock the door, we turn a handle to open it, we turn the water tap on and off, we turn a knob to switch on the wireless or the T.V. set, and so on.

The door of a room turns through an angle.

The hands of a clock turn through an angle.

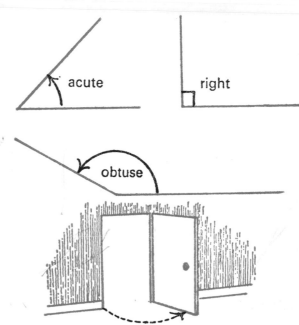

B

Fig 1

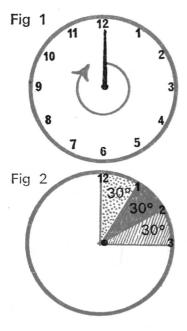

Fig 2

Let us look at the clock. When the minute hand moves exactly once round the clock, we say that it makes **one complete revolution.**

We know that the circumference of a clock face is marked off in 60 small divisions, called minutes. But let us imagine it is divided into 360 small divisions, which we call degrees. For short we write 360 degrees as 360°.

When the minute hand starts at 12 and reaches **the quarter past,** it turns through a quarter of a revolution, or 90°. ($\frac{1}{4}$ of 360° = 90°).

When it reaches **the half past,** it turns through half a revolution, or 180°. ($\frac{1}{2}$ of 360° = 180°).

When it reaches **the quarter to,** it turns through 3 quarters of a revolution. ($\frac{3}{4}$ of 360° = 270°).

Look at this drawing showing the minute hand moving to 5 past the hour, 10 past the hour, and 15 minutes past the hour. You can see that there are 3 large divisions between 12 and 3, so that the angle

turned through every 5 minutes,is 30°.
Now draw a full clock face, as
in Figure 3 and mark in the hours.
Join each division to the centre.

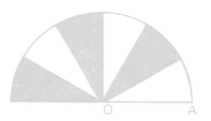

Fig. 3

As we saw the angle between the
lines in each division is 30°.

1. Through how many degrees does the
   minute hand turn in:

   (a) 5 min   (f) 40 min
   (b) 15 min   (g) 45 min
   (c) 20 min   (h) 50 min
   (d) 25 min   (i) 1 hour?
   (e) 30 min

2. If the minute hand turns through the following degrees, how many
   minutes have passed?

   (a) 30°   (b) 60°   (c) 90°   (d) 180°   (e) 210°   (f) 270°   (g) 300°

3. What fraction of a revolution (360°) does the minute hand turn in:

   (a) 10 minutes   (b) 15 minutes   (c) 20 minutes   (d) 30 minutes?

C In figure 4 you will see a drawing of the top part
   of figure 3 with the hour hand figures left out.
   Trace this figure on a piece of tracing paper,
   or greaseproof paper.

   How many degrees are shown in each coloured division?

You can use your tracing to measure angles in this way.

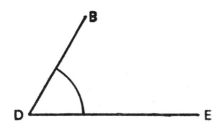

Here is an angle BDE.
D is the vertex

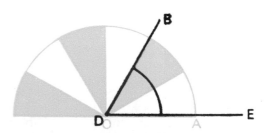

Place your tracing so that O is on
top of the point D and the line
OA lies along DE

You should find that the angle BDE is 60°.

36

1. Now use your tracing in this way to find the size of these angles.
Remember the size of an angle depends only upon how much one line
opens away from the other line. The length of the lines has **nothing**
to do with the size of the angle.

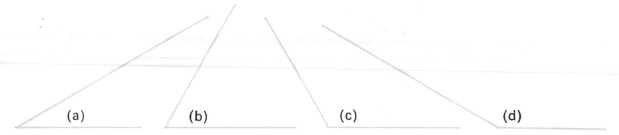

(a)   (b)   (c)   (d)

2. We made a Compass Card, like this,
with a square. Use a square of
tracing paper to copy this figure.

Each of the angles marked with a
dot is equal.

(a) How many angles are there?
(b) If they all add up to 360°, what
is the size of each angle?
(c) Use the above figure, which you
have traced, to measure the size of
these angles in degrees:

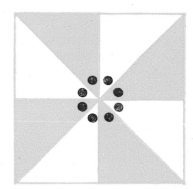

(a)   (b)   (c)

3.

Look at the points of the compass.
How many degrees does a weather vane pass
through in turning from:

(a) N to E   (b) E to S   (c) N to S   (d) W to N
(e) N to NE (f) NE to SE (g) SE to SW (h) NW to SW
(i) E to SE (j) W to NW (k) N to SE (l) S to NW?

Parallel Lines

A Look at the lines below.

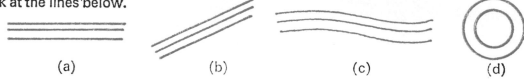

(a)   (b)   (c)   (d)

What can you say about the lines in each case?
Use a strip of paper to mark the distance between each pair of lines.
Do you find that the distances between the lines are always the same?
Lines which are always the same distance apart are said to be PARALLEL.
The lines in your exercise book are parallel.
The top and bottom edges of this book are parallel.
The two sides of your book are parallel.
Railway lines are parallel. Why?
Now point out to your teacher examples of straight lines in your
classroom which are parallel.

In the following drawings point out sets of parallel lines.

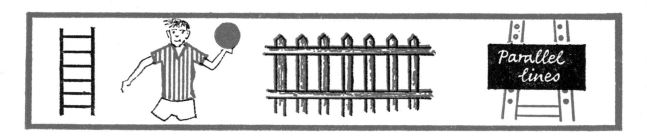

Can you point out (a) vertical parallel lines? (b) horizontal parallel lines?
(c) oblique (sloping) parallel lines?

B1. Place a ruler horizontally across your exercise
book and draw a line on each side of your ruler.

2. Now place your ruler vertically across these
2 lines, and draw a line along each side of your ruler.

    (a) What shape have you drawn in the middle?
    (b) Which lines are parallel?

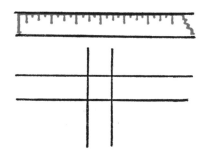

38

3. Draw 2 parallel lines horizontally along each side of your ruler.
Now slope your ruler across these 2 lines and draw a line on each
side of your ruler.
What shape have you drawn in the middle?

4. Again draw 2 parallel horizontal
lines. This time place 2 rulers
vertically across them and draw
lines along each side.
What shape have you drawn in the middle?

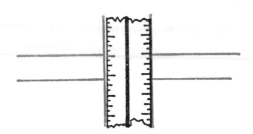

5. Draw your horizontal lines as above. Place 2 rulers at a slope
and draw 2 lines along the outside.
What is the shape in the middle called?

C

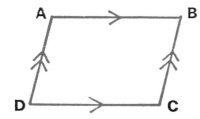

The fact that lines are parallel can be shown
in a figure.
Here the single arrow shows AB parallel to DC.
The double arrow shows AD parallel to BC.

Copy these shapes on squared paper and put in arrows
like these to show which lines are parallel.

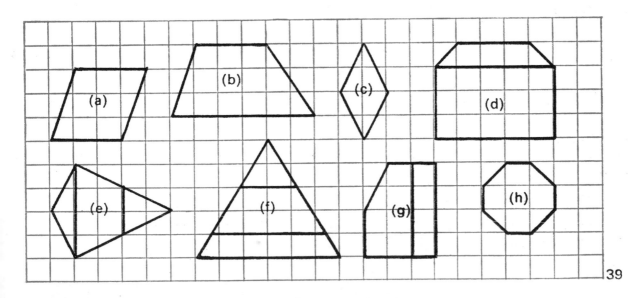

Sometimes, we want to show a drawing of solid figures.
Here you can see how to make drawings of three solids on squared paper.
In each figure copy the pattern of the small squares.

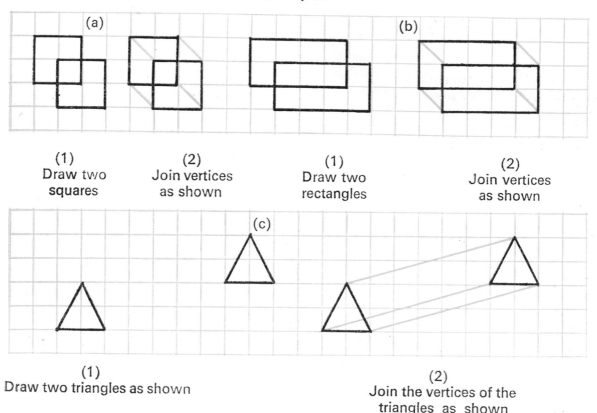

| (1) Draw two squares | (2) Join vertices as shown | (1) Draw two rectangles | (2) Join vertices as shown |

(1) Draw two triangles as shown

(2) Join the vertices of the triangles as shown

1. Give a name to each shape.

2. Each shape has some parallel lines. When you have drawn each shape on squared paper, use different colours to show parallel lines, like this:

   (a) The horizontal lines AB, DC, EF and HG are parallel. Colour each in RED.
   (b) The sloping lines AD, BC, EH and FG are parallel. Colour each in BLUE.
   (c) The vertical lines AE, BF, DH and CG are parallel. Colour each in GREEN.

   Shape (a)

   Now colour in the parallel lines in the other two solids in the same way.

3. In each solid point out lines which:

   (a) are parallel and vertical.
   (c) are parallel and sloping.

   (b) are parallel and horizontal.
   (d) form a parallelogram.

40

Set-squares

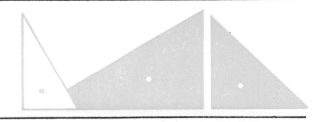

In Book 2 we used cardboard squares to draw perpendicular lines, which were parallel to each other, by sliding the square along the line. Setsquares are triangles of wood or perspex which we can use in the same way to draw right angles or parallel lines.

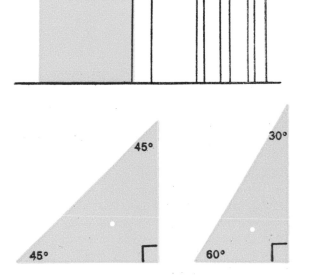

There are two kinds of setsquares.
Setsquare (a) has a right angle and two angles of 45°
($\frac{1}{2}$ of a right angle).
Setsquare (b) has a right angle, one angle of 60° and another angle of 30°.

A If you haven't any setsquares in your class, you can make them from cardboard in this way.

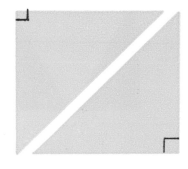

Join the opposite corners of a cardboard square (say 10 cm by 10 cm)

Cut along the dotted line

You now have two cardboard setsquares with one right angle and two angles of 45°.

41

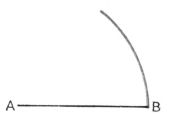

Draw on cardboard a line AB 8 cm long. Measure 8 cm on your compasses and with centre A draw a large arc.

With the same radius and centre B, draw another arc to cut the first arc at C.

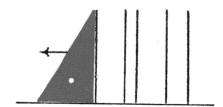

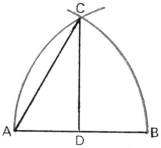

Mark the centre point of the line AB.
Call this point D.
Join point C to D, and A to C, to form a triangle.
Now cut out the triangle ADC, and use it as a setsquare.
(Angle at D = 90°, angle A = 60°, angle C = 30°).

B1. Draw a straight line. Place the bottom edge of your setsquare along the line and draw a line along the vertical edge. Slide your setsquare along the line and draw four or five vertical lines. These lines are all parallel to each other.

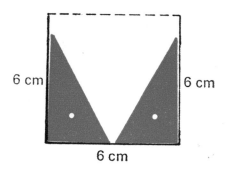

2. Draw a straight line 6 cm long. Draw perpendicular lines at each end with a setsquare. Mark points 6 cm up these vertical lines and join them, as shown. What shape have you made?

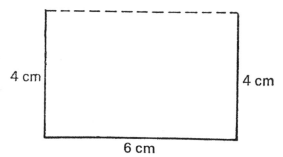

3. Now draw a line 6 cm long. Use your setsquare to draw perpendicular lines at each end. Measure 4 cm up these lines and join them as shown. What shape have you made?

42

4. Place two 45° setsquares together to make:

a square   a right-angled isosceles triangle

Place your two 60° setsquares to make:

a rectangle   an equilateral triangle   an isosceles triangle

Use two 45° setsquares and two 60°/30° setsquares to make a kite.

Use your setsquare to draw a T.V. aerial.

5.

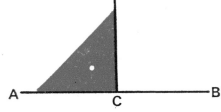

Draw a line AB 6 cm long.
At the mid-point C, draw a
perpendicular line.

Mark a point D 3 cm up.
Use your ruler to produce the
line DC to another point E, 3 cm down.
Join these points, as shown.

What shape is figure ADBE?

What kind of triangle is ADB?

How many congruent triangles do you see?

If you had made CE 5 cm long, what shape would the figure ADBE have been?

The Rhombus and Kite

Make a square with four equal Meccano strips, or geo-strips, or milk straws.

Push it sideways, like this, and you have a rhombus.

A 1. What can you say about the sides of a square?
2. Can you say the same thing about the sides of the rhombus?
3. Are the angles of the rhombus different from the angles of the square? In what way?

B Take a paper rectangle and fold it once down the middle, longways. Fold again across the middle. Join the two corners by a straight line. Cut along this line and open out. You now have a rhombus shape and four triangles left over.

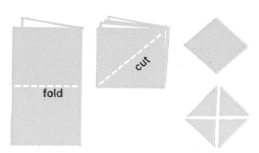

1. How could you prove that the shape is a rhombus?
2. Can you fit the four "left over" triangles to make a rhombus?
3. Can you place these four triangles on top of each other so that they fit exactly over each other?
4. Are the four triangles congruent?
5. Can you fit the four triangles exactly over your rhombus?
6. What does this tell us about the diagonals of a rhombus?
7. Use your paper right-angle, or a setsquare, to see if these four triangles are right-angled triangles.
8. What can you now say about the four angles at the centre of a rhombus?
9. Use your ruler or your four "left over" triangles to find whether the diagonals of a rhombus are equal. What did you find?
10. Is each diagonal of the rhombus a line of symmetry?

Fold your rhombus about the long
diagonal, as shown. What do you find
about the angles marked?

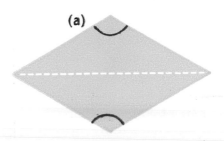

(a)

(b)

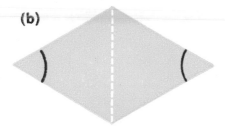

Now fold about the short diagonal.
What do you find about the
angles marked?

You can see that the marked angles in
shape (a) are opposite each other,
and the marked angles in shape (b)
are opposite each other.

What can you now say about the "opposite" angles of:

   (a) a rhombus   (b) a square   (c) a rectangle?

Copy these sentences into your exercise book and fill in the missing words.

   The . . . . of a rhombus are all equal.
   The opposite . . . . are equal.
   The diagonals of a rhombus are . . . . equal.
   The diagonals of a rhombus bi . . . . t each other at r . . . . t angles.
   Each diagonal of a rhombus is a line of sy . . . . y.

Here is a very easy way to draw
a rhombus.

(a) Place your ruler on your exercise
    book and draw along the
    outside edges.
(b) Now slope your ruler across
    these lines and again draw along
    the outside edges.

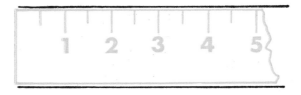

The shape in the middle is a rhombus.

Why?

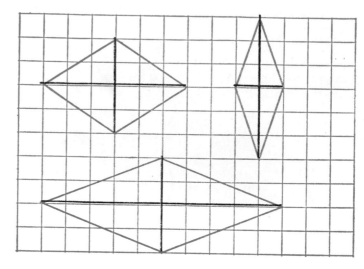

C Draw these rhombuses in your squared paper book, and then draw some of your own.
It is always a good plan to draw the diagonals first.

D The Kite

Have you ever flown a kite like the one at foot of the page? Kites are of different shapes, but most are in the shape of the one in the picture.

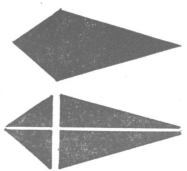

Fold a paper rectangle, longways, along the middle. Mark a point about $\frac{1}{4}$ of the way from the end. Draw straight lines from this mark to the corners. Now cut along these lines.

You should now have a kite shape and four triangles left over.

1. Can you place the four triangles together to make another kite shape?
2. Is this kite congruent to the other kite?
3. Place the two smaller triangles on top of each other.
   Do they fit exactly?   Are they congruent?
4. Do the same with the two larger triangles.
   Do they fit exactly?   Are they congruent?
5. Are the four triangles right-angled triangles?
6. In what way is the kite different from the rhombus?
7. Are the diagonals of the kite the same length?
8. Fold your kite shape about the longer diagonal.
   Do the two halves fit exactly?
9. Now fold it about the shorter diagonal.
   Do the two halves fit exactly?
10. Which diagonal is the line of symmetry?
11. Which sides of the kite are equal?
12. Which angles are equal?

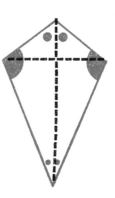

46

E In your squared paper book draw a
  square like this, 12 squares long
  and 12 squares broad.

  Draw a line up and down the middle.
  Call this line AC.

  Draw another line across the middle.
  Call it BD.

  Mark the points shown on the vertical
  line and letter them, as in the
  drawing.

  Join each point to B and D.
  In the drawing we have joined
  G to B and D, and E to B and D.

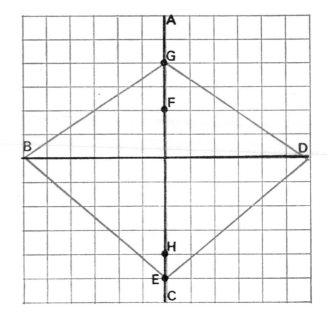

What shape does this make?

Now make more kites by joining each point in the vertical line
to B and D.

Join points on AC to B and D to make a rhombus.

Join points in the same way to make a square.

F Copy these shapes on squared paper.

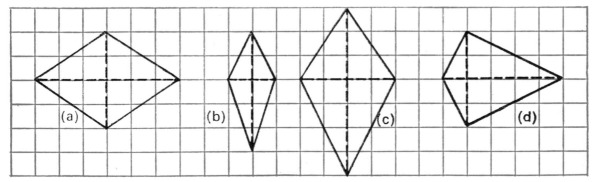

1. Find the area of each shape (in box units).

2. Can you find a short way of finding the areas?

3. With a coloured pencil draw in any lines of symmetry.

4. Point out any pairs of congruent triangles.

47

Area

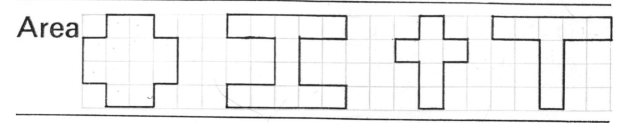

A. We learned in Book 2 that the area of a figure is the number of squares in it. The squares, of course, must all be the same size.

Copy the shapes above on squared paper and in each write the number of squares in it.

The size of square we use for finding the area of small surfaces, such as a page of this book or your desk, is the CENTIMETRE SQUARE.

What is the length of each side of this square?

We say that the area of this square is a SQUARE CENTIMETRE.

The shorthand way of writing **square centimetre** is cm².

B 1. Get a **10 cm** square of thin cardboard and divide it off into centimetre squares as shown in this drawing. Cut out these centimetre squares.

(a) How many cm squares have you?

(b) What is the area of each square?

(c) What then is the area of a 10 cm square?

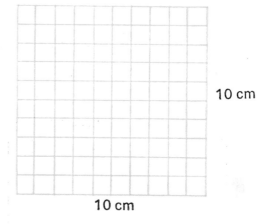

2. Cover each of the shapes below with centimetre squares and so find the area of each shape in cm²

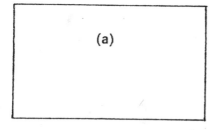

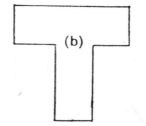

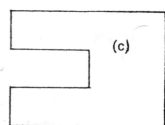

The squares in the figures at the top of the page are smaller than centimetre squares. If they were centimetre squares, what would be the area of each shape in cm²?

3. Use 16 of your cm squares each time to form:

      (a) a square   (b) a rectangle   (c) 3 more shapes of your own

What is the area in cm² of each shape?

4. Do you see from this that the area of a figure does not depend on its shape, but on the number of square units (in this case cm²) in it?

   (a) How many coloured dots are there in the rectangle on the right?
   (b) How many small squares are there?
   (c) Can you find a quick way of counting the number of small squares?

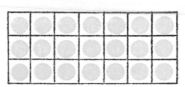

5. In the shapes below each small square stands for a square in which each side is 1 centimetre. So each small square stands for 1 cm².

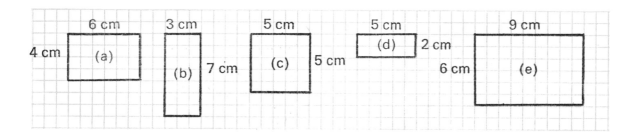

   (1) How many cm squares are there in each shape?

   (2) What is the area of each shape in square centimetres (cm²)?

6.

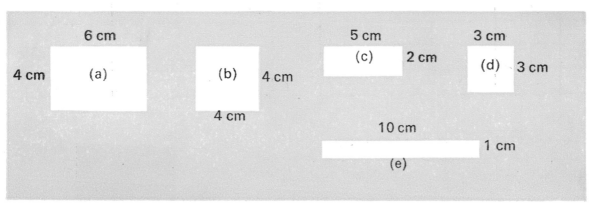

Above are some shapes, but the small squares have been left out. The length and width of each are shown in cm. Find the area of each shape in square cm.

7. Count the number of squares in this rectangle.
There are 18.
If each of these squares stands for a square cm,
we can say that the area of the rectangle is
18 square centimetres.
The length of the rectangle is 6 cm.
What is the width? It is 3 cm.
So clearly the width is (18 ÷ 6) cm.

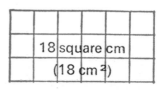

18 square cm
(18 cm²)

6 cm

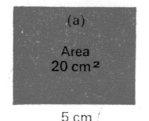

(a)

Area
20 cm²

5 cm

(b)

Area
8 cm²

2 cm

(c)

Area
9 cm²

3 cm

(d)

Area
20 cm²

4 cm

Can you now see a quick way of finding the width of these rectangles?
Find the width of each and say how you found it.

8. A class drew 12 rectangles. In the tables below you are given two
facts about each rectangle. Copy the tables and put in the third
measurement. The first has been done for you in each table.

	Length	Breadth	Area
(1)	8 cm	7 cm	56 cm²
(2)	6 cm	5 cm	
(3)	10 cm	6 cm	
(4)	5 cm	4 cm	
(5)	9 cm	3 cm	
(6)	12 cm	6 cm	

	Length	Breadth	Area
(7)	6 cm	4 cm	24 cm²
(8)	7 cm		35 cm²
(9)		4 cm	32 cm²
(10)		3 cm	30 cm²
(11)	6 cm		12 cm²
(12)		2 cm	14 cm²

C If you used 1 cm squares, you would need a
large number of them to cover the top of a table,
or the floor of your class room.
So we need larger measures.

We can use a square which has all
its sides 10 cm long.
How many cm² are there in this square?

10 cm

10 cm

50

For still larger surfaces we can measure in metres (m)
and square metres (m²)

If each side of a square is 1 metre, then the area of
the square is 1 square metre (1 m²).

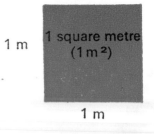

1 m | 1 square metre (1 m²)

1 m

To get a good idea of the size of a square metre, place
4 metre sticks on the floor in the form of a square.

Use a metre stick to draw a 1 metre square on the blackboard
and estimate (guess) the approximate area of the blackboard
in square metres.

Do the same on the floor and estimate its area in square metres.

	Length	Breadth	Area
(a)	3 m	4 m	
(b)	5 m	5 m	
(c)		4 m	20 m²
(d)	6 m		18 m²
(e)	6 m		36 m²
(f)		8 m	72 m²
(g)	8 m		56 m²
(h)	12 m	10 m	
(i)	4 m	1½ m	
(j)		12 m	144 m²

Copy this table into your exercise
book and fill in the missing
measurements.

D We saw that the diagonals of a square and of a rectangle divided the
shape into two equal triangles. Each triangle, then, is half of the
square or rectangle:

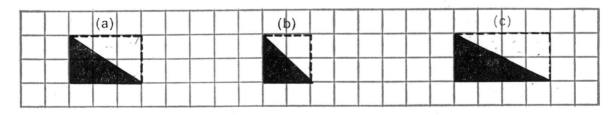

(a) Area = ½ of 6 boxes
  = 3 boxes

(b) Area = ½ of 4 boxes
  = 2 boxes

(c) Area = ½ of 8 boxes
  = 4 boxes

51

1 If each small box stands for **1** square cm, what is the area of each triangle in square cm?

2. If each small box stands for **1** square metre, what is the area of each triangle in square metres?

3. Find out the areas of these shapes, if each small box stands for **1** square cm. The dotted lines will help you.

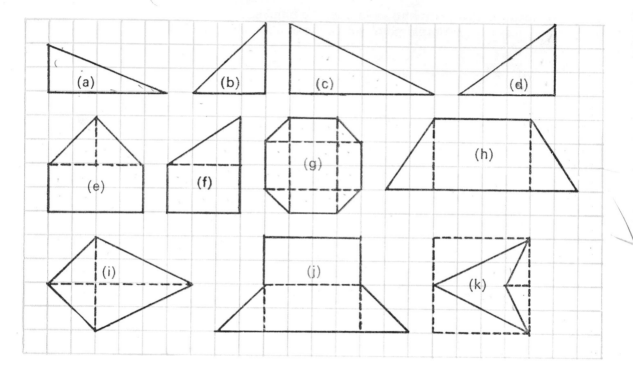

E Some shapes such as circles, leaves or coins, cannot be divided into squares or half squares.

Look at this shape. It shows the outline of a leaf drawn on squared paper.
Each small square stands for a square cm.
It would be hard to find the exact area of the leaf, but we can get fairly close to its area in this way:

(a) Count the whole squares inside the leaf.
(b) Count as a whole square any part which is more than half a square. These are shaded.
(c) Do not count at all any part smaller than half a square.

So the area of this leaf is about 25 small squares, that is, the area of the leaf = 25 square cm. (25 cm².)

1. Now, in the same way, find the approximate area of these shapes, and find out which has the smallest area, and which the largest.
Each small square stands for 1 square cm.

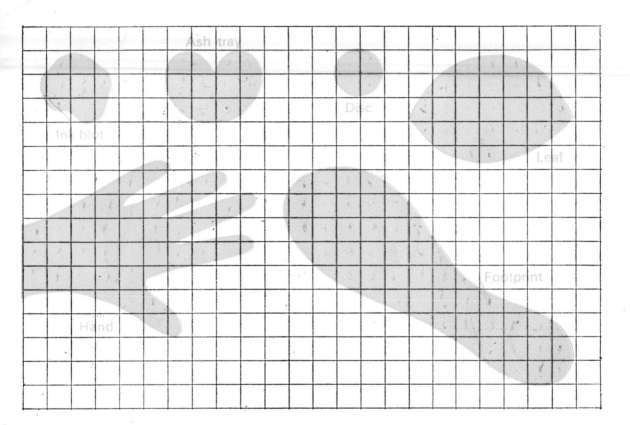

2. On squared paper marked off in square centimetres draw 2 circles of any size you please. Count the number of square cm in them and so find the approximate area of each circle.

You could draw the circles by tracing round the top of a tumbler, or cup, or any other round object.

3. Draw some shapes of your own on 1 cm squared paper and find their approximate area.

You could find in this way the area of:
(a) your hand   (b) your foot   (c) a coin
(d) the top of a teacup   (e) an ink blot you have made
(f) a leaf from a tree   (g) a dinner plate   (h) a lollipop.

Scales and Plans

In books and comics you see drawings
of people, cars, buildings and so on.
These cannot be drawn the same size
as they are, unless you use a huge
sheet of paper.
When we make them smaller in drawings,
each part of the drawing has got
to look the same, as if we were
looking at it from a distance, and
not like drawing (b).
Each part of the drawing has to be
made smaller in the same way.
What is wrong with drawing (b) ?

We could not draw lines of 50 cm or 100 cm in our books, but we
could make 1 cm stand for 50 cm or for 100 cm, or for any
other length. We call this the SCALE of our drawing.
If you look at a map you will see the scale to which it is drawn.

One map might have this scale: 1 cm to 100 km, or 1 cm/100 km

Another map might have this scale: 1 cm to 300 km (1 cm/300 km)

A1. Here are some lines. Measure them with your ruler:

(a) _____   (d) _____
(b) _____   (e) _____
(c) _____   (f) _____

Write down in your exercise book the length of each line.

2. What does the length of each line stand for, if the scale is:
(a) 1 cm to 10 cm   (b) 1 cm to 20 cm   (c) 1 cm to 50 cm   (d) 1 cm to 1 m?

3. Here are some pictures.

Measure the length and height of
each of these drawings.
If the scale is 1 cm to 10 cm, what
is the real length and the
real height of the articles?

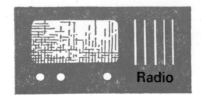

54

Bookcase

STEREO

Record Player

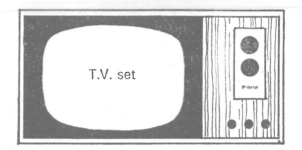

T.V. set

4. Look at this picture:

(a) Measure the length and height of the van in cm and $\frac{1}{2}$ cm.
(b) Measure the height of the flag-pole in cm.
(c) Measure the height of the boy in cm.
(d) Find out how long the boat is, and what its height is in cm.
(e) If the scale of this picture is 1 cm to 120 cm, find out what each of these lengths and heights are in metres and centimetres.

Write your measurements, like this:

	Size of drawing		Real size	
	Length	Height	Length	Height
Van				
Flagpole	—		—	
Boy	—		—	
Boat				

5. Here is a smaller drawing, or a **scale drawing** of a house and a garden. We are looking **down** on the garden from above.

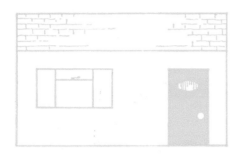 

The scale is 1 cm to 1 m (100 cm). Measure in cm and $\frac{1}{2}$ cm.

(a) How long is the real house?

(b) How high is the real house?

(c) How wide is the door?

(d) How long is the window?

(e) How high is the window?

(f) How long is the real garden?

(g) How wide is the real garden?

(h) How long is the vegetable patch?

(i) What is the real length of each side of the drying green?

(j) How wide is the real flower bed?

6. Here are some boys and girls standing in front of a fence.

(a) If Bill is 150 cm tall, what is the scale of the drawing?

(b) How tall is Ann?

(c) What height is little Mary?

(d) How much shorter is Ann than Bill?

(e) What height is Tom?

(f) By how much is he taller than Jean?

(g) By how much is he taller than the dog?

(h) Who is twice as tall as the dog?

56

The Circle

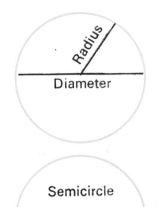

Radius

Diameter

Semicircle

Quadrant

We have already seen that:

The **circumference** is the distance all round a circle, or the boundary line of a circle (the coloured line in this drawing).

The **radius** is the distance from the centre to the circumference. Any straight line from the centre to the circumference is a radius.

The **diameter** is the distance from the circumference, through the centre, to the circumference. Any straight line drawn from the circumference to the circumference, through the centre, is a diameter. The radius of any circle is half the diameter.

All **radii** of the same circle are equal.

A **semicircle** is a half circle.

A **quadrant** is a quarter circle.

1. Using compasses to draw circles

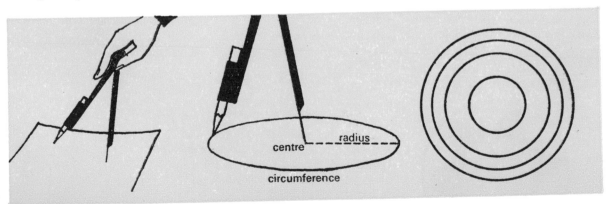

centre — radius

circumference

Open the compasses a little, about 3 cm or so. Stick the metal point into the paper and hold compasses at the top.

Keep the pencil on the paper and trace out the circle with the pencil.

Open the compasses more and more each time. Keep the same centre and draw more circles.

2. Sometimes we need to draw a circle whose radius is a certain length. Let us draw a circle of radius 3 cm. What is its diameter?
Use your ruler and open the legs of the compasses 3 cm. Keep the compasses fixed at this radius and draw a circle.
Now draw circles of radius $2\frac{1}{2}$ cm, $3\frac{1}{2}$ cm, and 4 cm.

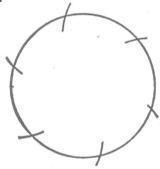

Again draw a circle whose radius is 3 cm. Keeping the same centre, draw circles of radius $3\frac{1}{2}$ cm, 4 cm, $4\frac{1}{2}$ cm, as shown in this drawing, to make a target. Colour the target. Circles which have the same centre are called *concentric* circles.

3.

Draw a circle of 3 cm radius. Mark a point on the circumference. Keeping your compasses open 3 cm, mark off the circumference into six equal parts.

Join the six points and you have a shape called a
regular hexagon.

Draw three diameters, as shown here, and you have six triangles. What kind of triangles are they? Why?

Draw a circle. Mark off the six points of the regular hexagon, and then join them, as in this drawing, to make a star. Colour the star in your own way.
See if you can make other designs, using the six points of the regular hexagon.

Here is a design you could try to copy. You may find it difficult at first, but keep trying until you have copied it perfectly. Colour it.

4. Using compasses to draw an **equilateral triangle**

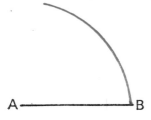

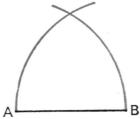

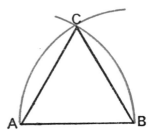

Draw a straight line AB 4 cm long. Open the legs of the compasses 4 cm, and with centre A draw a large arc. (An arc is just a part of the circumference.)

Keep the legs of the compasses open 4 cm, and with centre B draw another arc to cut the first arc at the point C.

Draw straight lines from C to A and B. Why is the triangle you have drawn an equilateral triangle?

5. Drawing an **isosceles triangle**

Draw a line AB 4 cm long. Open your compasses 5 cm, and with centre A draw an arc. Keeping the legs of the compasses open 5 cm, and with centre B draw another arc to cut the first arc. Mark this point C. Draw lines from C to A and B. Why is the triangle an isosceles triangle?

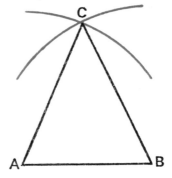

6. Designs with circles

Study these designs to see how they are drawn and then copy them. Invent some designs of your own.

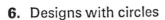

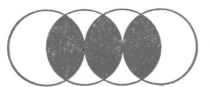

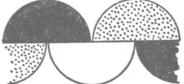

Shapes make Shapes

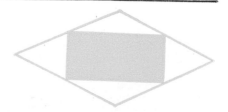

1. Draw in your squared paper book a
   square of sides 6 cm. Mark the middle
   points of each side and join these points
   by straight lines, as shown in the drawing.
   It is a good idea to use different colours
   of pencil.

2. What do you think this new shape is?

3. Now put a dot where you think the mid-point
   of each side of this new shape is, and join
   them up, as shown.

4. Continue joining the mid-points of each new shape.

   (a) What do you find about each of these new shapes?
   (b) Can you point out sets of parallel lines
       in the shapes?

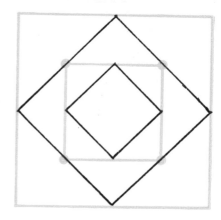

5.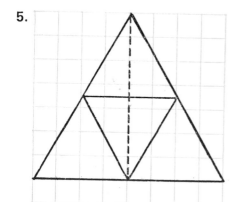

   Measure the sides of this triangle.
   What kind of triangle is it?
   Draw the triangle in your squared paper book, using
   the same number of squares. Mark the mid-point of
   each side and join them as shown.
   What can you say about each of the four triangles
   you have drawn?
   Point out any lines which are parallel and any
   angles which you think are equal.
   Join up the mid-points of the new triangle you made.
   What do you find about this new shape?

6. Copy these drawings, using the same
   number of squares.
   Join the mid-points
   of each shape to make
   another shape.
   What do you find about each new shape?

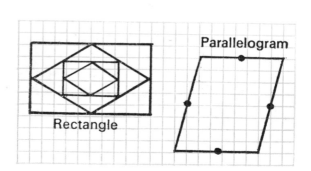

Rectangle

Parallelogram

60

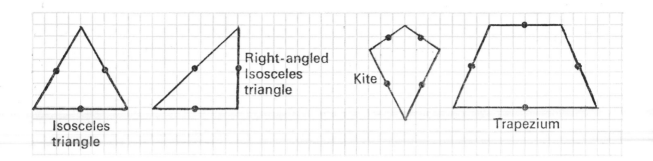

Isosceles triangle

Right-angled Isosceles triangle

Kite

Trapezium

7.

Take a 10 centimetre cardboard square. Mark the mid-points of each side.
Draw the horizontal line, dividing the square into two equal parts.
Mark the mid-point of this line.

Now draw the four sloping lines. Cut along the horizontal line, so that you will have two rectangles. Now cut along the sloping lines. You should now have 6 pieces.

(a) What name do we give to each of the pieces with sloping sides?
(b) What name do we give to each triangle?
(c) Use 2 triangles to make a square.
(d) Use 2 triangles to make another triangle.
 What kind of triangle is it—equilateral, isosceles, or scalene?
(e) Use 2 triangles to make a parallelogram.
(f) Use 3 triangles to make a trapezium.
(g) Use 4 triangles to make a square.
(h) Use 4 triangles to make a parallelogram.
(i) Use 4 pieces to make a rectangle.
(j) Put the 6 pieces together again to make a square.
(k) Using some or all of your pieces, make as many symmetrical shapes as you can.

Symmetry

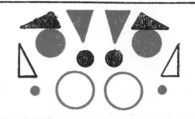

We have seen how some shapes can be divided into two equal parts by a line or a fold, called a **line of symmetry**. Look at these shapes with lines of symmetry dividing the shape into two equal or **congruent** parts.

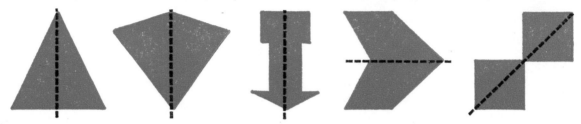

The lines of symmetry can go in any direction. Where would you put a line of symmetry in each of the pictures below? Point it out with your pencil.

1. Here are some half shapes with a line of symmetry shown. Copy these shapes into your exercise book and draw in the other half to make a symmetrical figure.

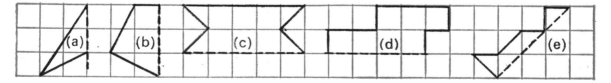

2.

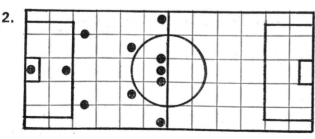

Here is a drawing of a football pitch, and the players of one team shown by **11 black dots. Copy this drawing** and place dots of another colour in the other half of the drawing to show the other team lined up in the same pattern.

3. Here are some patterns:

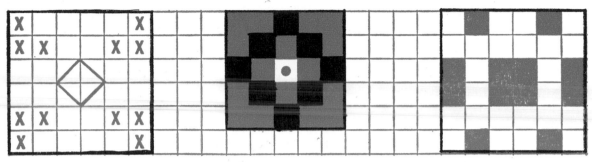

Stitch Pattern   Linoleum Pattern   Crossword Pattern

Copy these patterns above into your exercise book.
Can you find any lines of symmetry in the patterns?
Draw in any you can find with dotted lines.
Turn your exercise book so that the top is on your right.
Do all the patterns still look the same as the ones above?
Which two are different?
Now turn your exercise book so that the top is now at the bottom.
What do you find?
Now turn it once again so that the top is now on your left.
What do you find about each pattern?

4.

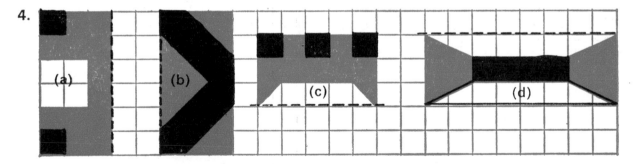

Above are some half patterns. Draw them and fill in the other half
to make a symmetrical figure. Find out which ones remain the same
when turned round as before?

5. Now take some paper shapes or
counters and try to arrange them in
symmetrical patterns.

6. Look at papers and magazines and cut out any pictures which are
symmetrical. Perhaps you could paste them into a "Book of Symmetry"
or put them on a poster to show in your classroom.

7. Make a list of things around you which are symmetrical.

Which of these do you think are symmetrical:
- (a) a T.V. set
- (b) a vase
- (c) a butterfly
- (d) you
- (e) a pair of shoes
- (f) a clock
- (g) a cricket bat
- (h) a penny?

8. Some shapes show more than one line of symmetry. For example we found that the square had four such lines (shown by the dotted lines).

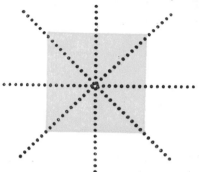

You remember we tested this by folding about the dotted lines, and we found that each half, when folded about the line, exactly fitted the other half.
Test this by folding a paper square about the lines shown.

9. Now look at these shapes and find out how many lines of symmetry each figure has. Copy each figure, dot in any lines of symmetry, and below each write the number of such lines.

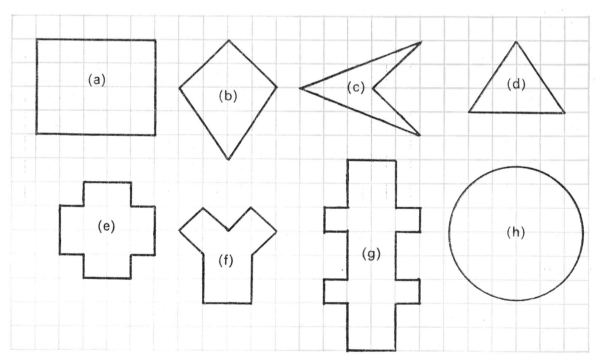

64

Sets

We have seen that sets are collections of things—objects, animals, men, numbers—in fact a collection of any number of things. The things that make up a **SET** are called **members** or **elements** of the set—that is, they **belong** to the set.

Here is a set of flowers found in Britain.

F = {rose, daffodil, tulip, iris, pansy, daisy, violet, lily}

Notice:

(1) We have used a sort of 'code' name (F) for the set. We can use any capital letter to stand for any set. We chose F (for flowers). This saves us time writing.

(2) The members of the set are written in curly brackets, and are separated by commas.

(3) We always state clearly what the set is. (Some flowers could not be included in the set as, although they are flowers, they are not found in Britain). Can you think of some such flowers?

1. What are the members of the following sets? Write them down in curly brackets like the set of flowers.

S = the coins in common use in Britain.
A = the first six letters of the English alphabet.
O = the months of the year beginning with O.
E = the first four even numbers.

2. Look at these sets: A = {1, 2, 3, 4, 5}

B = {2, 4, 6, 8}

C = {3, 6, 9, 12}

We could say that A is the set of whole numbers less than 6, and that B is the set of even numbers less than 10.

What about set C? We can say that C is the set of whole numbers less than 13 which will divide evenly by 3.

Now see if you can say what these sets are:

D = {1, 2, 3, 4, 5, 6, 7, 8}   G = {4, 8, 12, 16}

E = {2, 4, 6, 8, 10}   H = {1, 3, 5, 7, 9}

F = {3, 6, 9, 12, 15}   I = {5, 10, 15}

3. Look at this set B = {Tom, Dick, Harry}

What is this set? We don't know because we are not told.
It could be a set of footballers, or runners, or policemen, or baby boys. Can you think of other sets to which they might belong?
In this case B is the set of red-haired boys in Class 5.
So we must say clearly what set we are looking at.

4. Here is another set: G = {Jean, Alice, Mary, Nan}.

Write the set down, and after it write a set to which these could belong.

5. Write these sets down in the proper way with a code letter, and see
if you can describe them in words. Remember you can use any capital
as a code letter.

(a) cup, saucer, plate.   (d) March, May.

(b) lion, tiger, wolf.   (e) Spring, Summer, Autumn, Winter.

(c) Saturday, Sunday.   (f) Hammer, chisel, spanner, saw.

Instead of writing out in full, "poodle is a member of the set
of dogs", we use a sort of shorthand and write:

Poodle ∈ {dogs} **The symbol ∈ means "is a member of"**

So January ∈ {months} is short for "January is a member of the
set of months".

6. Now write the following in the same way:

(a) Dog is a member of the set of animals.
(b) Canary is a member of the set of birds.
(c) Tiger is a member of the set of cats.
(d) 4 is a member of the set of even numbers.
(e) 9 is a member of the set of odd numbers.

7. What do these mean?

(a) England ∈ {countries}   (d) Oak ∈ {trees}

(b) Clyde ∈ {Scottish rivers}   (e) Collie ∈ {dogs}

(c) Tennis ∈ {games}   (f) 6 ∈ {even numbers}

8. Here are some members of sets and below them some sets. Find out to what set each member belongs, and write down your answer in the short way, like this: Cup ∈ {Dishes}.

TREES	NUMBERS	FRUIT	ANIMALS	
SPORTSMEN		TOOLS	BIRDS	BOATS

9. Look at these sets:

$$A = \{2, 4, 6, 8\} \qquad B = \{3, 5, 7, 9\}$$

2 is a member of set A, so we could write 2∈A.
7 is a member of set B, so we could write 7∈B.

Write down the other members of both sets in the same way.

10. If we want to say that an object, or a number, is NOT a member of a particular set, we simply write down the symbol ∈, and cross it out, like this—∉

∉ means "is not a member of"

So we write:

Peter ∉ {girls}   Turnip ∉ {flowers}   Elephant ∉ {birds}

5 ∉ {even numbers}   8 ∉ {odd numbers}   ½ ∉ {whole numbers}

Look at the sets below and then write in this way an object which is **not** a member of the given set.

A is a set of chairs.   B is a set of tools.
C is a set of footballers.   D is a set of wild animals.

11. State whether these "shorthand" sentences are true or false. (Write T or F)

(a) Rose ∉ {Vegetables}   (g) 12 ∉ {odd numbers}
(b) Robin ∈ {fish}   (h) Glasgow ∈ {French cities}
(c) Sparrow ∈ {British birds}   (i) Betty ∈ {Boy scouts}
(d) Sam ∉ {Girl Guides}   (j) Scone ∉ {meat dishes}
(e) $\frac{7}{8}$ ∈ {fractions} (k) Triangle ∈ {quadrilaterals}
(f) 23 ∈ {even numbers}   (l) Square ∉ {circles}

12. A set can mean "things we are talking about". Suppose we are talking about the kinds of fish. Then, clearly, we are not talking about horses, or sweets, or birds.

We can show this by drawing a ring round the "members which belong to" the set we are talking about, and leaving things which are not members of the set outside the ring.

Suppose we are talking about the set of farmyard animals (Code F). We could show this in a drawing, like this (with other things which do not belong to the set outside the ring).

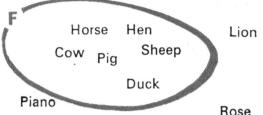

Note that the "ring" has members of the set we are talking about inside it.

So we can say Cow ∈ F and Rose ∉ F.

13. Here is a list of things. Copy this list into your exercise book in the same order as shown. Then draw a ring round those which belong to the set of Clothes (C).

Below write a list showing (with symbols ∈ and ∉) the members which belong to set C and the members which do not belong to set C.

Handkerchief	Coat	Frock	Vest	Cap
Slippers	Trousers	Jacket	Blouse	Sandshoes
Umbrella	Shirt	Jersey	Skirt	Handbag

14. Here is a list of numbers. Copy these numbers, as shown here, into your exercise book. Then draw a ring round those which belong to the set of even numbers (E) and write a list below (in the proper way) of the numbers which belong to set E, and those which do not belong to it.

```
        15      17
  23    2   8   50   10
  41   16   4   12   18
        7   9   11
```

In the same way we can show members of a Set. Suppose Class 5 has boys and girls in the class. We can show this by using rings. Call the set of children in Class 5, set F.

We can show all the children in set F by a large ring, and the boys in set F by a smaller ring inside. What do you think the coloured part would stand for? Clearly, the rest of set F, that is, the girls.

15. Here are some sets:

S = {Smith family}   A = {animals}   N = {numbers}

Draw a large ring for each set with the "code-name" shown as above. Now draw a smaller ring inside the large ring to show these smaller sets.

(a) Bob and John Smith   (b) Fractions   (c) Dogs

Numbers from Numbers

Here you see some patterns you can make on a peg board or with counters, or with large dots in your exercise book.

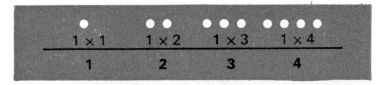

1×1	1×2	1×3	1×4
1	2	3	4

Here we count in **ones**
1, 2, 3, 4 are called
MULTIPLES of **1**

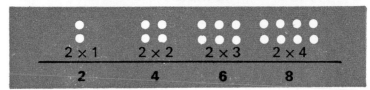

2×1	2×2	2×3	2×4
2	4	6	8

Here we count in **twos**
2, 4, 6, 8 are called
MULTIPLES of **2**

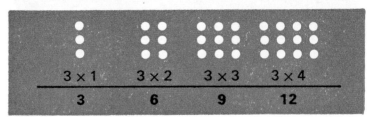

3×1	3×2	3×3	3×4
3	6	9	12

Here we count in **threes**
3, 6, 9, 12 are called
MULTIPLES of **3**

To find multiples of **1**, you write down **1**, and add **1** each time.
To find multiples of **2**, you write down **2**, and add **2** each time.
To find multiples of **3**, you write down **3**, and add **3** each time, and so on.

The first eight multiples of 2 = 2, 4, 6, 8, 10, 12, 14, 16
For short we could write $M_2 = \{2, 4, 6, 8, 10, 12, 14, 16\}$
M_2 stands for "multiples of 2".

1. Now in the same way, write down the first eight multiples of:

    3   4   5   6   7   8   9   10

2. Here is part of your multiplication square.

×	1	2	3	4	5	6
1	1	2	3	4	5	
2	2	4	6	8		
3	3	6	9			

Draw the multiplication square on squared paper.
Continue the square up to 10.
You will see that in each row we have multiples of 1, 2, 3, 4, 5, 6, etc.
Does each column show the same multiples?

3. Use your square to write down in your exercise book the first 10
   multiples of the set of numbers {1, 2, 3, 4, 5, 6, 7, 8, 9, 10}

   Remember that, for short, M_1 = the set of multiples of **1**
   M_2 = the set of multiples of 2

   The first two are done for you:
   $$M_1 = \{1, 2, 3, 4, 5, 6, 7, 8, 9, 10\}$$
   $$M_2 = \{2, 4, 6, 8, 10, 12, 14, 16, 18, 20\}$$

   Continue in this way up to M_{10} (multiples of 10)

   If you look at your multiplication square (up to 10 × 10), you will see
   that 12 is a multiple of 2, a multiple of 3, a multiple of 4, and a
   multiple of 6.
   (The number 12 appears in row 2, row 3, row 4 and row 6)
   Here is 12 shown in "dot" patterns.

4. Now look again at your multiplication square (up to 10 × 10).
   Write down numbers of which these are multiples:

   (a) 8   (b) 16   (c) 20   (d) 24   (e) 30   (f) 32   (g) 36
   (h) 54   (i) 60   (j) 64   (k) 70   (l) 72   (m) 80   (n) 90

5. Write down all the numbers up to 100 which are multiples of 2, 3, and 4.

6. Many things are sold in multiples.

   Shoes and socks are sold in multiples of 2.
   Cups and saucers are usually sold in sixes.
   Cigarettes are sold in multiples of 5—5, 10, 20, 50 and so on.

   Can you tell your teacher of any sweets and other things which
   are sold in multiples?

Look at these multiples of 2 and of 3.

$M_2 = \{2, 4, 6, 8, 10, 12\}$ $M_3 = \{3, 6, 9, 12, 15, 18\}$

You will see that the multiples of 2 can be divided evenly by 2.
And the multiples of 3 can be divided evenly by 3.
So the multiple of any number can be divided evenly by that number.

For example: 12 is a multiple of 3
$12 \div 4 = 3$ — — — 12 is a multiple of 4
$12 \div 6 = 2$ — — — 12 is a multiple of 6

7. Here is a set of numbers: $\{12, 15, 18, 21, 24, 27, 30, 33, 36\}$

Which of these numbers are multiples of:

(a) 2   (b) 3   (c) 4   (d) 5   (e) 6   (f) 7   (g) 8   (h) 9   (i) 10

8. Write down numbers of which each of these numbers is a multiple.
(You can use your 10×10 multiplication square).

(a) 24   (b) 36   (c) 28   (d) 56   (e) 72   (f) 84

9.

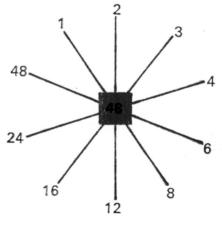

In the small square is the number 48.
You can see that 48 can be divided
evenly by each of the numbers shown.
So 48 is a multiple of each of
these numbers.

Show, in the same way, the numbers of which these are multiples:

(a) 18   (b) 24   (c) 36   (d) 42   (e) 54

Counting Bases

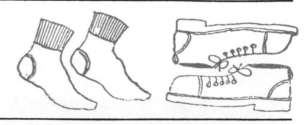

A We usually count in TENS, since we have 10 fingers.
Look at these abacus pictures, where we learned to count in tens.

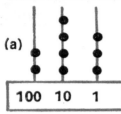

(a)

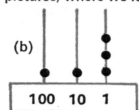

(b)

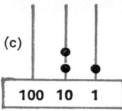

(c)

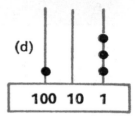

(d)

1. In (a) we see that $243 = (100 \times 2) + (10 \times 4) + (1 \times 3) = 200 + 40 + 3.$

2. Write down in this way, the abacus number shown in (b).

3. In (c) we see that $21 = (100 \times 0) + (10 \times 2) + (1 \times 1) = 20 + 1$

4. Write down, in this way, the abacus number shown in (d).

5. Draw some more abacus pictures to show "ten count" numbers, and write down what each number really means.

B We often use other numbers to count in, besides 10.
Shoes and socks are sold in **2**'s—we count in twos.
Cups and saucers are usually sold in **6**'s—we count in sixes.

1. What numbers are usually used to count cigarettes?

2. What units of time are counted in: 7's, 24's?

3. In what sports are players counted in: 2's, 4's, 11's, 15's?

4. Find out how chalks are counted by counting the number of chalks in a box.

C Place 13 counters in a row, like this: ● ● ● ● ● ● ● ● ● ● ● ● ●

1. If we want to count in TENS, we can count these as "1 ten and 3 odd ones (3 units)."
Divide them into a 10 and a 3, and draw an abacus picture to show this.
(We can say we are "COUNTING IN LOTS OF 10" (or counting in BASE 10.)

2. We can also count these 13 counters in other ways.
Divide your 13 counters as shown, copy the table, and
fill in any missing spaces.

	DIVISION OF COUNTERS	COUNTING BASE (LOTS)	NUMBER OF LOTS	UNITS LEFT
a)	●●●●●●●●● ●●●●	9	1	4
b)	●●●●●●●● ●●●●●	8	1	5
c)	●●●●●● ●●●●●● ●	6		1
d)	●●●●● ●●●●● ●●●	5		
e)	●●●● ●●●● ●●●●●			
f)	●●●●●●●●●●● ●●			
g)	●●●●●●●●●●● ●			

D

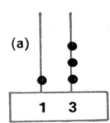 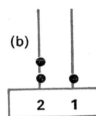 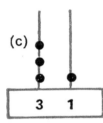

(a)   1   3   (b)   2   1   (c)   3   1

(a) When we used the abacus, we were counting in TENS (or BASE 10).
Here 13 (base 10) is shown in 3 ways, counting in **10**'s in **6**'s and in **4**'s:
$13 = (10 \times 1) + (1 \times 3) = (6 \times 2) + (1 \times 1) = (4 \times 3) + (1 \times 1)$

(b) Draw some abacus pictures, like these, to show 13 counted in bases 9, 8, 5 and 12.

When we count in 10's, we say that $13 = 13_{TEN}$ (which we read as "one-three, base 10").

This means   1 ten + 3 units

When we count in 9's, we say that $13 = 14_{NINE}$ (which we read as "one-four, base 9").

This means   1 nine + 4 units

Since 1 ten + 3 units = 1 nine + 4 units, $13_{TEN} = 14_{NINE}$

(a) Write down in this way 13_{TEN} in counting bases: 8, 6, 5 and 4.

(b) Arrange 15 counters in a row, and divide them to show that
you are counting in bases: 10, 9, 8, 6, 5 and 4.

(e) Make a table, and draw abacus pictures to show these numbers.

(d) Write down 15_{TEN} .in the other counting bases.

Number Patterns

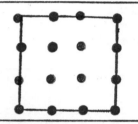

Here are some dot patterns which you can draw, or make with pegs on peg board, or make on your desk with counters.

A

Dot pattern				
Number of dots from the top down	1	1 + 2	1 + 2 + 3	1 + 2 + 3 + 4
Total	1	3	6	10

These numbers—1, 3, 6, 10 are called Triangular Numbers. Why?
Write down the next 3 triangular numbers, arrange them in dot patterns, and write down the numbers in each row of dots from top to bottom.

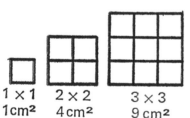

B If each small square in these patterns stand for 1 square cm, you can see that:

1×1 2×2 3×3
$1 cm^2$ $4 cm^2$ $9 cm^2$ $? cm^2$

What area is the next larger square?
We can show this in a dot pattern.

Dot pattern				
Number of dots	1	1 + 3	1 + 3 + 5	1 + 3 + 5 + 7
Total	1	4	9	16

74

These numbers—1, 4, 9, 16 are called Square Numbers. Why?
Write down the next 3 Square numbers, arrange them in dot patterns, and
write down the area of each square in this way—2 × 2, 3 × 3, 4 × 4 and so on.
These dot patterns show us an easy way to add odd numbers in order:

1	$= 1 = 1 \times 1 = 1^2$	The first odd number is 1 or 1^2
$1 + 3$	$= 4 = 2 \times 2 = 2^2$	The sum of the first 2 odd numbers is 2^2
$1 + 3 + 5$	$= 9 = 3 \times 3 = 3^2$	The sum of the first 3 odd numbers is 3^2
$1 + 3 + 5 + 7 = 16 = 4 \times 4 = 4^2$		The sum of the first 4 odd numbers is 4^2

Find in this way the sum of:

(a) The first 5 odd numbers   (b) The first 8 odd numbers
(c) The first 10 odd numbers   (d) The first 20 odd numbers

C Here are the first 5 Triangular numbers and the first 5 Square numbers
in this pattern:

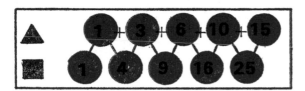

You can see each pair of
Triangular numbers adds up
to a Square number.

A dot pattern makes this clear:

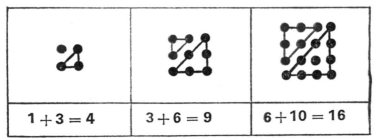

$1 + 3 = 4$	$3 + 6 = 9$	$6 + 10 = 16$

In these 2 ways find out the
6th and 7th square and
triangular numbers, and show
by a dot pattern how these
two Triangular numbers
make up a Square Number.

D Some numbers can be made up in a rectangular dot pattern.

2 and 3 multiplied make 6   2 and 4 multiplied make 8

2 and 3 are called Factors of 6   2 and 4 are called Factors of 8

What is the next rectangular number? What are its factors?

75

Here are several ways we can "make up" the number 12

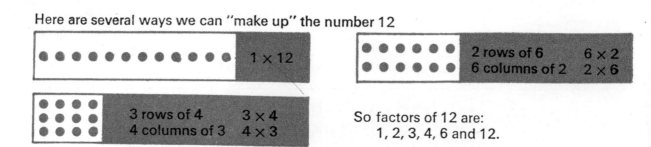

So factors of 12 are:
1, 2, 3, 4, 6 and 12.

Notice that **12** can be divided evenly by each of its factors.
Now arrange these numbers in dot patterns and find the factors of
each number: 16   18   20   24

E Try to "make up" square or rectangular dot patterns for these:

2   3   5   7   11   13

You should find you cannot make a square or rectangle dot pattern for them.
Numbers which cannot be arranged to make up a square or rectangle dot
pattern are called **PRIME NUMBERS.**

Now add 4 more prime numbers to the set of primes:

{2,   3,   5,   7,   11,   13,   —,   —,   —,   — }

Number Sentences

Look again at a part of the addition table.

+	0	1	2	3	4	5	6
0	0	1	2	**a**	4	5	6
1	1	2	3	4	5	6	7
Row 2	2	**b**	4	5	6	7	**c**
3	3	4	**d**	6	7	8	9
4	4	5	6	7	**e**	9	10
5	5	6	7	8	9	10	11
6	6	7	8	9	**f**	11	12

Column

By using row and column we can add:
$3+4=7$ and $4+3=7$

We can also use the table to subtract:
$7-3=4$ and $7-4=3$

A1. Look at the table and say what number each letter stands for.

2. Write and complete the following:

(a) $\mathbf{a}-3=$ (b) $\mathbf{b}-2=$
(c) $\mathbf{b}-1=$ (d) $\mathbf{c}-2=$
(e) $\mathbf{c}-6=$ (f) $\mathbf{d}-3=$
(g) $\mathbf{d}-2=$ (h) $\mathbf{f}+6=$

B Now look at these mathematical sentences:

$5+3=8$ $6+4=10$ $7-2=5$

You can see that in each sentence one side is equal to the other side. Sentences like these are called **equations.**

1. Write down 6 equations of your own from the table.

Now look at this equation: $\mathbf{n}+4=9$
Would the statement be true if we put 7 in place of **n**?
Would it be true if we put 5 in place of **n**? Of course, it would.
Would it be true if we put any other number in place of **n**?
So the statement is true only if we put 5 in place of **n**.
We say, then, that $\mathbf{n}=5$.

2. What numbers can be put in place of **n** in these equations?

(a) $\mathbf{n}+2=6$ (b) $\mathbf{n}+3=10$ (c) $\mathbf{n}-5=11$ (d) $\mathbf{n}-7=5$
(e) $\mathbf{n}+6=14$ (f) $\mathbf{n}-10=10$ (g) $\mathbf{n}+5=12$ (h) $\mathbf{n}-8=6$

It is useful to compare an equation with a pair
of scales that are balanced.
Here we have 6 kg on each side of the scales.
So the scales are evenly balanced.
The equation is: $4 + 2 = 6$.

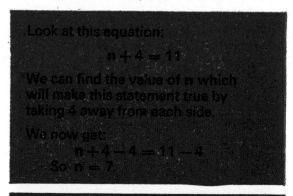

If we added 2 kg to one side only, what would happen?
Clearly, to keep the balance, we must add 2 kg
to the other side.

If we added 7 kg to one side, what must we add to the other side
to keep the balance?

If we took 2 kg off one side, what must we do to the other side to
keep the balance?

If we doubled the weight on one side, what would we have to do to
the other side to keep the balance?

It is clear that to keep the balance we must treat both sides in the same way.

Look at this equation:

$$n + 4 = 11$$

We can find the value of n which
will make this statement true by
taking 4 away from each side.

We now get:

$$n + 4 - 4 = 11 - 4$$
So $n = 7$

3. By taking away the same number
   from each side find what **n**
   stands for in the following equations:

   (a) $n + 2 = 3$ (b) $n + 3 = 5$
   (c) $n + 4 = 7$ (d) $n + 5 = 8$
   (e) $n + 6 = 10$ (f) $n + 7 = 15$
   (g) $n + 9 = 17$ (h) $n + 10 = 19$

Look at this equation:
$$y - 6 = 3$$
Add 6 to each side
$$y - 6 + 6 = 3 + 6$$
So $y = 9$

4. Find in this way what **y** stands
   for in these equations:

   (a) $y - 2 = 7$ (b) $y - 3 = 5$
   (c) $y - 1 = 7$ (d) $y - 4 = 8$
   (e) $y - 5 = 1$ (f) $y - 6 = 14$
   (g) $y - 7 = 18$ (h) $y - 8 = 20$

5. Here are some equations of each kind. Find in each case what number
   the letter stands for:

   (a) $y + 2 = 12$ (b) $n - 4 = 9$ (c) $a + 4 = 13$ (d) $b - 7 = 9$

   (e) $c - 2 = 18$ (f) $y + 9 = 13$ (g) $n + 5 = 17$ (h) $y - 11 = 20$

   (j) $n + 7 = 15$ (k) $y - 6 = 10$ (l) $c + 4 = 20$ (m) $a - 9 = 30$

Graphs

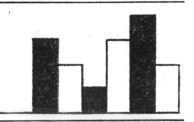

You have learned how "box pictures", or graphs, as they are called,
can give information about things at a glance.

Here is such a graph showing the amount of pocket money that
7 children have. Beside it is a second graph in which straight
lines only are used, giving the same information. Straight line graphs
are very easy to draw.

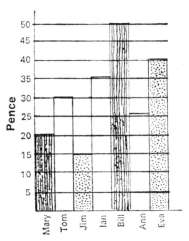 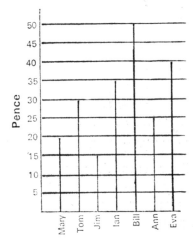

1. Use the graphs to answer these questions:

    (1) Who has the most money?

    (2) Who has the least?

    (3) How much more has Eva than Mary?

    (4) How much less has Jim than Ian?

    (5) How much have the three girls between them?

    (6) How much have the four boys altogether?

2. Draw a line graph of your own, like the second one above, to show the
amount of money each of these children has.
Jack 45 p   Fred 20 p   Pat 40 p   Lucy 35 p   Pam 15 p   Enid 50 p

3. In 4 weeks Mr. Jones bought the following quantities of petrol for his car:
1st week 35 litres   2nd week 40 litres   3rd week 30 litres   4th week 25 litres
Draw a graph to show this.

4.

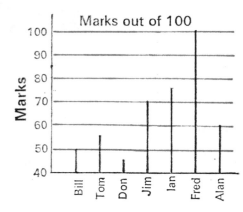

Marks out of 100

This graph shows the marks of 7 boys in an examination. Since no boy scored less than 40, we can start the marks column at 40.

(a) Who had the highest mark?

(b) Who had the lowest mark?

(c) How many more marks had Fred than Bill?

(d) Write down the marks in order, starting with the highest mark.

(e) Add up all the marks and divide this by 7. This gives the average mark.

(f) Which boys were above the average and which were below the average?

5. Here are the marks scored by 10 girls.

Jean	May	Ann	Meg	Kate	Eva	Rita	Sue	Enid	Lena
70	85	60	50	95	45	75	70	65	55

Draw a line graph to show these marks. Now make up some questions about the graph, like those above, and ask your neighbour to answer them.

6. Here is a graph with the lines across the page.

DISTANCES JUMPED BY 10 BOYS
AT THE SCHOOL SPORTS

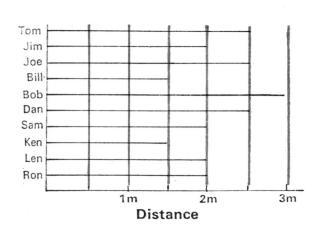

Distance

(a) What length (in cm) does each small division stand for?

(b) Who won, and how far did he jump?

(c) Who jumped less than 2 metres?

(d) Who tied for 2nd place, and how far did they jump?

(e) How much further did Ron jump than Ken?

(f) How many centimetres were the three boys who came second short of the winning jump?

(g) What was the difference in length between the longest and the shortest jump?

7. Mark a chalk line in your playground in metres (as in the graph above) and note the distances boys and girls can jump. Then draw a graph to show this.

80

3. Here is another kind of graph:

 stands for 2 cakes.

 stands for 1 glass of lemonade.

Tom's Party

(a) Who had the most lemonade?
(b) Who ate most cakes?
(c) How many more cakes did Betty eat than Jean?
(d) How many cakes were eaten at the party?

(e) Who drank the least lemonade?
(f) How many glasses of lemonade were drunk at the party?
(g) If lemonade was 3 p a glass and a cake cost 2 p, how much was spent on lemonade and cakes?

9. A sweetshop takes the following money:

Day	Mon	Tues	Wed	Thur	Fri	Sat
Money in £s	30	15	35	40	55	60

Draw a vertical line graph to show this, and then ask your neighbour some questions about it.

0. Here are some distances some children live from Glandale School. The distances are given in metres.

Jim	Mary	Tom	Betty	Bill	Jean	Joy
300	450	50	200	300	550	150

Draw a horizontal line graph to show this.

1. Here are the points won by 6 football teams last season. Draw a picture graph to show this. Let ● stand for 5 points.
Make up some questions about your graph and see if your neighbour can answer them.

Carrick Rovers	45 points	Southbank	20 points
Western United	40 points	Oldcastle	20 points
Scotia Thistle	25 points	Whitepool	15 points

Solids

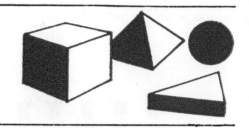

A1. Look at these solids

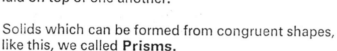

(a)   (b)   (c)   (d)

We saw that each of these shapes could be made from
congruent shapes, like those on the right,
laid on top of one another:

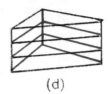

Solids which can be formed from congruent shapes,
like this, we called **Prisms.**
Which of the solids below are prisms?

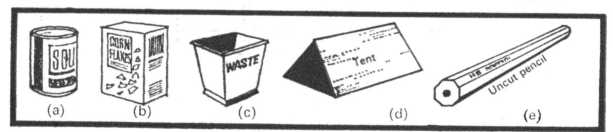

(a)   (b)   (c)   (d)   (e)

What kind of solid is each prism?
What shape is each of the shapes shaded?
What solids could you make from: a pack of cards, a pile of records
all the same size, a number of pennies, a pile of these books?

B We saw that some shapes had
flat surfaces, and some had
curved surfaces.

The cover of your exercise book laid flat on your desk is a flat surface.
Curl it up and the top and bottom are both curved surfaces.

Here are some drawings.

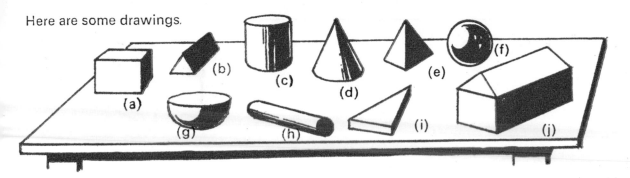

1. Which of the above solids have only flat surfaces?
2. Which of the above shapes has only curved surfaces?
3. Which shape has 6 flat surfaces?
4. Which shapes have 5 flat surfaces?
5. Which shapes have 2 flat surfaces and 1 curved surface?
6. Which shapes have 1 flat surface and 1 curved surface?
7. What solids make up solid (j) above?
8. Which of these solids are prisms?
9. Which solids touch the table at only one point?
10. Which solid touches the table along one straight line?

1. Try to stand each of these upright on a flat level surface:
   a match, a drinking straw, a pencil, a piece of chalk.
   It is not very easy, is it? Can you say why?

2. Now place a match box on a flat level surface.
   You can place it in 3 different ways. Try to blow
   the match box down each time. You should find that
   with the match box in one position it was
   very hard to blow down. What position?
   Can you say why it is harder?

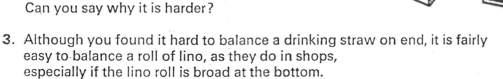

3. Although you found it hard to balance a drinking straw on end, it is fairly
   easy to balance a roll of lino, as they do in shops,
   especially if the lino roll is broad at the bottom.
   The broader the base, the easier it is.

4. A ball will roll easily since it only touches the ground at one point.

5. If a cylinder is laid with its curved surface on a
   flat table, it touches the table only along one
   line. So it is easy to roll it. But if it is placed
   upright, it touches the table over a wider area,
   and so it is harder to push.
   Can you now say why it was harder to blow over
   the match box in one position?

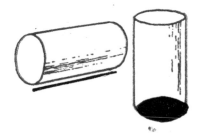

Skeleton Solids

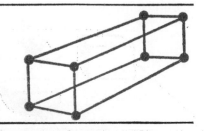

A Look at an OXO cube or any other cube.
How many faces has it?
When it is placed on a table, how many faces lie
on the table?

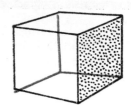

How many faces are at right angles to the table?
How many faces are parallel to the table?

Let us make a "skeleton" of a cube with straws.
How many straws will meet at each corner? How many corners are there in a cube?
How many links shall we need?

This is how we make a link to join 3 straws.

Bend a piece of pipe
cleaner, like this, and
press the two parts
firmly together.

Now bend again
to make a T shape.

Bend back one
of the arms to make a
right angle.

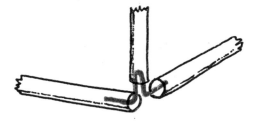

Now use the link to join
3 straws together, as shown
in this diagram.

Use more links to complete the **skeleton** of the cube.
(a) How many corners are in your skeleton cube?
(b) How many straws are in it?
(c) How many edges are there in a cube?
(d) What is the shape of each face of a cube?

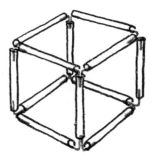

B Making a skeleton cuboid

Take 4 whole straws, 4 half straws and 4 straws
about a third the length of a whole straw.
Make links as before and join up your straws
to make the skeleton of a box or cuboid.

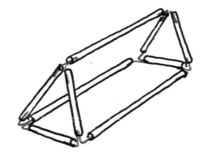

1. How many corners has a cuboid?
2. How many faces?
3. How many faces lie on the table?
4. How many faces are at right angles to the table?
5. How many faces are parallel to the table?
6. In what ways is a cuboid like a cube?
7. In what ways is it different from a cube?
8. Name some things which have the shape of a cuboid.

C Making a triangular prism.

Use three whole straws and six half straws to make
the triangular prism as shown:

1. Where do you often see this shape?
2. How many corners has it?
3. How many faces has it?
4. What shapes are the faces?
5. How many edges has it?

D Here are two other ways to make "skeletons"

1. Cocktail sticks and "blobs" of
   plasticene.

2. Knitting needles and corks.

Volume and Capacity

A You all know what a cube is. Above are some cubes you often see.

Here is a cube like those some young children use to help them to count. Each side is 1 cm long.

How many sides (or faces) has a cube? Count them carefully—don't count the same one twice.

Collect some small wooden cubes. If you can get 1 cm cubes, so much the better. If your cubes are bigger than 1 cm cubes, never mind. Just imagine they are 1 cm cubes.

Using your 1 cm cubes, build another cube with each side 2 cm long.

How many cubes do you need? 8, of course.

Build another cube with sides 3 cm long.

How many cubes did you need this time?

Was it a lot more than you thought?

Look again at what we did when we made the 2 cm cube.

(a) We wanted it to be 2 cm long. So we put 2 cubes side by side.

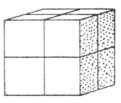

(b) We wanted it to be 2 cm wide. So we put 2 cubes behind the first 2 cubes.

We now had $(2 \times 2) = 4$ cubes

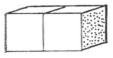

(c) We wanted it to be 2 cm high. So we put another layer of 4 cubes on top of the first layer.

We now had $(2 \times 2 \times 2) = 8$ cubes

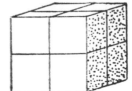

When we made the 3 cm cube we needed to take:

(a) 3 cubes side by side.

(b) 3 more cubes behind the first and then another 3 behind these.
     So we had 9 cubes (3 lines of 3).

(c) 3 layers, each of 9 cubes—$9 \times 3 = 27$ cubes.

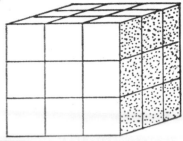

In Book 2 we learned that:

2×2 can be written in shorthand as 2^2 (we say "two squared").

In the same way $2 \times 2 \times 2$ can be written as 2^3 (we say "two cubed").

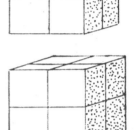

1. Now read these shorthand numbers and write the number each stands for:

(a) 1^2 3^2 5^2 10^2 (b) 1^3 4^3 5^3 10^3

The numbers you found for (a) are called **square numbers.**

The numbers you found for (b) are called **cubic numbers.**

Each small cube you have been using is a centimetre cube.

We say that the centimetre cube has a **volume** of 1 cubic cm.

The volume of any object is the amount of space it takes up.

The short way of writing **1 cubic cm is 1 cm³.**

3 centimetre cubes take up 3 cubic centimetres of space
So their volume is 3 cm³.

2.

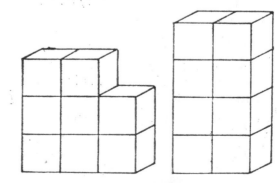

Here are 8 cm cubes arranged in two more ways.
Arrange your 8 cubes in as many ways as you can.
What is the volume of each cube?
What is the volume of each shape you have made?
So the volume of an object does not depend on
its shape but on the number of cubic units in it—
that is, on the amount of space it occupies.

B We have already learned in Book 2 that the **volume** of a bottle, or jug, or any other container, is the amount it can hold when full.
The volume of any container used for holding **liquids** can be measured in LITRES.

| This jug holds 1 litre | This milk bottle holds $\frac{1}{2}$ litre | This wine bottle holds $\frac{3}{4}$ litre (0·75 litre) | This bucket holds 5 litres |

Sometimes we want to know the volume of a container for holding **solids.**

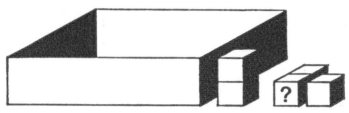

To measure the volume in such cases we find out how many **cubic centimetres** the box will hold.

Look back to the previous page where we built up cubes of different sizes, using centimetre cubes.

If you can get a hollow centimetre cube you can use it to find the volume of other containers.

Fill your centimetre cube with dry sand and empty it into a match box. Go on filling and emptying it till the match-box is full. In this way find how many **cm³** of sand the box can hold.

It would be a slow business if we had to fill boxes with dry sand from a centimetre cube every time we wanted to know how much they could hold.

There is a much easier way.

The drawing shows a number of cm cubes neatly arranged in the form of a rectangle. You can see that:

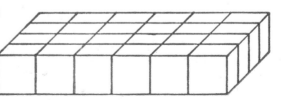

(1) there are 6 cubes in each row.

(2) there are 4 rows.

(3) there are 6 × 4 = 24 cubes altogether.

1. Imagine this is a plastic box completely filled with cm cubes.

   (a) How many cubes are there in each layer?

   (b) How many layers are there?

   (c) How many cubes are there in the box?

   (d) How many cm cubes can the box hold?

   (e) What is the volume of the box (in cm^3)?

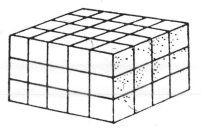

2.

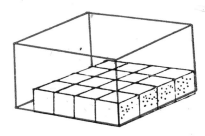

Here is a box 5 cm long, 4 cm wide and 3 cm high. It is to be filled with cm cubes.

   (a) How many cubes are already in the box?

   (b) How many more cubes can be put in the bottom layer?

   (c) If another layer of cm cubes were put into the box, would the box now be full?

   (d) How many more layers of cm cubes could be put into the box?

   (e) How many cm cubes altogether can be put into the box?

   (f) What is the volume of the box (in cm^3)?

3. Here is an empty box.

   (a) What is the length, the breadth and the height of the box?

   (b) How many cm cubes would be needed to fill the bottom?

   (c) How many layers would fill the box?

   (d) How many cm cubes could the box hold?

   (e) What is the volume of the box?

   (f) Imagine the box is 10 cm long, 6 cm wide and 4 cm high.

      (1) How many cm^3 of dry sand could it hold?

      (2) How many cm^3 of sugar could it hold?

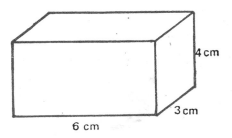

4 cm

3 cm

6 cm

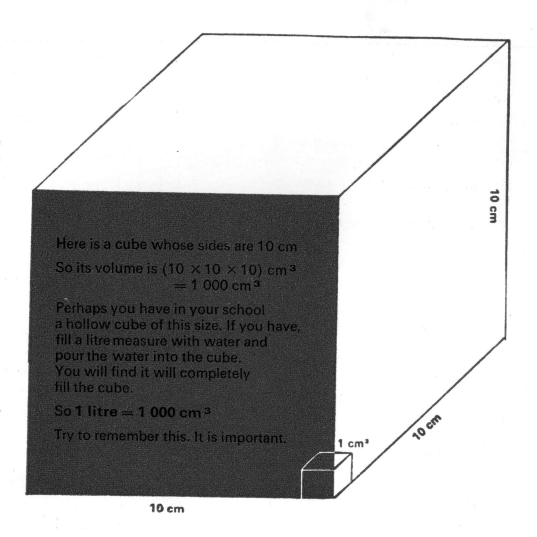

Here is a cube whose sides are 10 cm

So its volume is (10 × 10 × 10) cm³
$$= 1\ 000\ cm^3$$

Perhaps you have in your school
a hollow cube of this size. If you have,
fill a litre measure with water and
pour the water into the cube.
You will find it will completely
fill the cube.

So 1 litre = 1 000 cm³

Try to remember this. It is important.

1 cm³

10 cm

10 cm

10 cm

10 cm

Fill a 10 cm hollow cube with dry sand and then empty it on to
the table. You'll be surprised at the amount (volume) of sand.
Once again you can see that the volume is the same, though the
shape has changed.

4. How many cm³ of sand can be put into a 5 litre bucket?

5. If 1 litre of water weighs 1 kg, what it the weight of 1 cm³ of water?

6. The fish tank in Tom's classroom is 40 cm long,
25 cm wide and 10 cm high. How many
litres of water will it hold when filled to
the brim?

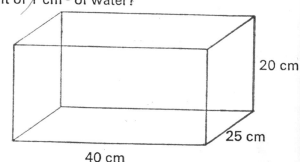

20 cm

25 cm

40 cm

Making Sure

1. What number is half way between
$2\frac{7}{8}$ and $3\frac{1}{8}$?

2. A bus holds 32 people. How many buses are needed to take 440 pupils and 8 teachers on an outing?

3. John ate $\frac{1}{8}$ of a cake. Bill $\frac{1}{4}$ and Tom $\frac{3}{8}$. What fraction of the cake was left?

4. $(1 \cdot 4 + 0 \cdot 8) - (1 \cdot 4 - 0 \cdot 8) = $?

5. Add 3 more numbers to this set:
$\{0 \cdot 4, 0 \cdot 8, 1 \cdot 2, —, —, —\}$

6. How many grammes in:
$3\,kg + \frac{1}{2}\,kg + \frac{3}{4}\,kg$?

7. A grain store has 3 sacks of flour weighing 25 kg, 15 kg and 10 kg. How many $\frac{1}{2}$ kg bags can be made up from them?

8. A small tub of honey weighs 17·5 kg. Empty it weighs 1·5 kg.
  (a) What is the weight of the honey?
  (b) How many $\frac{1}{2}$ kg jars of honey can be filled from it?

9. A man works 8 hours a day for 5 days. If he earns $41\frac{1}{2}$ new pence an hour, what is his weekly wage?

10.

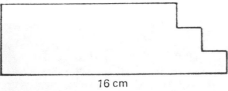

The "steps" are equal in height and in width. What is the perimeter of the figure?

B 1. A man earns £16 for a 40-hour week. What does he earn per hour?

2. A tube of 20 tablets weighs 14 grammes. When 10 tablets have been used, the weight is now 8 grammes. How many grammes does the tube weigh?

3.

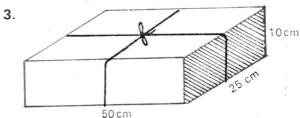

  (a) How many edges of the box measure
       50 cm   25 cm   10 cm?
  (b) Find the length of string used as shown, allowing 15 cm for knots.

4. 8 books, all of the same thickness, are put in a pile. If the pile is 36 cm high, how thick is each book?

5. A car travels 12 km on 1 litre of petrol. About how many litres are needed to cover 357 km?

6. How much change from £1 after spending 24 p, $38\frac{1}{2}$ p and $27\frac{1}{2}$ p?

7. How many packets each containing 250 g can be filled from 1 kg 750 g of sweets?

8. I bought 3 shirts and 2 ties for £3·95. Each shirt cost 95 p. What was the price of a tie?

91

Work Cards

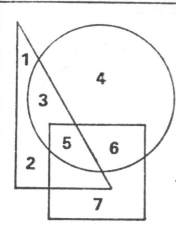

1.
1. Which number is in the circle only?
2. Which number is in the square only?
3. Which numbers are in the triangle only?
4. Which number is in the square and circle only?
5. Which number is in the circle and triangle only?
6. Which number is in each of the three shapes?
7. Is it true that the set of numbers {3, 4, 5, 6} are all in the circle?
8. Which members of this set are in the square?
9. Which members of the set are not in the triangle?
10. Now make up a drawing like this, or one of your own with different shapes. Put in some letters instead of numbers, and make up some questions for your neighbour to answer.

2.

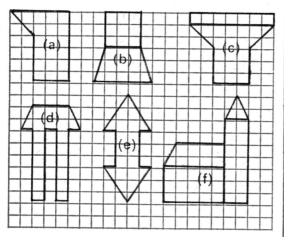

Copy these shapes in your squared paper book. Count the number of squares in each shape.
If your squares are cm squares, find the area of each shape in cm².

3.

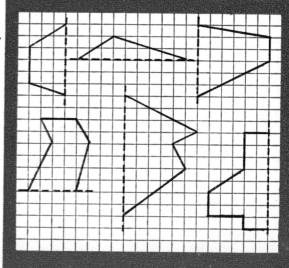

Draw these shapes in your squared paper book and then draw in the other half to make each a symmetrical shape. The dotted line is the line of symmetry.

92

4.

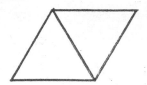 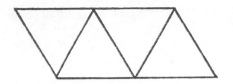

Draw an equilateral triangle on cardboard and cut it out. (If you can get one made of wood or plastic, you don't need to draw one.)
Draw round your triangle on coloured gummed paper to make a number of equilateral triangles. Cut these out and use them to make the shapes above. Stick the shapes into your Book of Shapes. Below each shape, write its name and also the number of equilateral triangles you used to make it.

5.

Copy these designs on squared paper. Continue them across the page and colour them in your own way. Name as many shapes as you can in each. Now make some designs of your own.

6.

6	+	?	−	1	= 8
×		+		+	
?	+	?	−	2	= 7
−		−		+	
1	+	?	−	?	= 9
= 5		= 2		= 4	

Draw this figure in your squared paper book.
Fill in the missing numbers to make a true number sentence in each row and column.

7. Draw this figure on a 10 cm cardboard square.
It will help you if you first measure along
5 cm from the corners, as shown.
Now cut along the unbroken lines and you will have:

  a square, a parallelogram
  a large triangle, 2 smaller triangles.

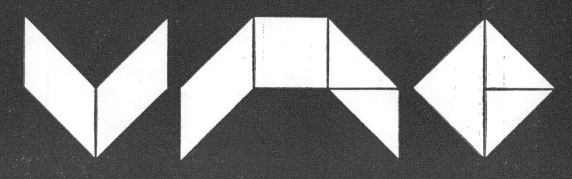

1. What kind of triangle is the large triangle?
2. What kind of triangle is each small triangle?
3. Use the two small triangles to make a
   triangle like the large triangle.
4. Use the two small triangles to make
   a parallelogram.
5. Close this book and use all the five pieces to make
   the large square in the drawing.
6. Use some or all of your five pieces to make symmetrical shapes.
   First make those shown below.

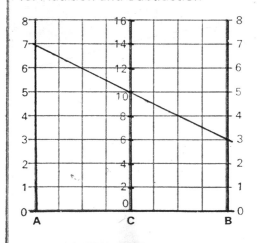

8. A NOMOGRAM
for Addition and Subtraction

Copy this **nomogram** on squared paper.

1. Place a ruler to join 7 on scale A
   to 3 on scale B. The ruler crosses
   scale C at 10, showing $7 + 3 = 10$.
   Use your ruler in this way to add
   other numbers.
2. Use your ruler to join 12 on scale C
   to 7 on scale A. The ruler crosses
   scale B at 5, showing $12 - 7 = 5$.
   Use your ruler in this way to
   subtract other numbers.
3. Add more numbers to the top of each
   scale and add and subtract
   more numbers.

1. In this pictograph each 🧍 stands for 20 people. What does 🧍 stand for?
How many people live in each of these five villages?

Eastway 🧍🧍🧍🧍🧍🧍🧍🧍

Weston 🧍🧍🧍🧍🧍🧍🧍🧍🧍🧍🧍

Garfang 🧍🧍🧍🧍🧍🧍🧍🧍🧍🧍🧍🧍

Hilton 🧍🧍🧍🧍🧍🧍🧍🧍🧍🧍🧍🧍🧍🧍🧍

Mostby 🧍🧍🧍🧍🧍🧍🧍🧍🧍🧍🧍🧍🧍🧍🧍🧍🧍

2. Draw a pictograph of your own to show the number of people living in these five villages.

Westbury 140   Melway 180   Southway 200   Alton 170   Galton 75

3. Using the symbol ◹ to stand for 10 houses, draw a pictograph to show the number of houses in these four streets.

Carrick St. 80   North St. 85   High St. 70   South St. 45

4. The different kinds of cars in a car park were counted.

Ford 24   Morris 16   Austin 14   Vauxhall 18   Hillman 20

Use a symbol of your own to stand for 4 cars and then draw a pictograph.

This is a circle of radius $3\frac{1}{2}$ cm.
Draw several this size. Measure with your compasses the length from 12 to 1 in the drawing on this page and use this distance to mark off the circumference, as shown. Perhaps an easier way is to mark off the distance from 12 to 1 on a paper strip and use this to mark off the circumference. By joining points you can draw different shapes. If you join points 8, 12 and 4, you will make a triangle. What kind of triangle?

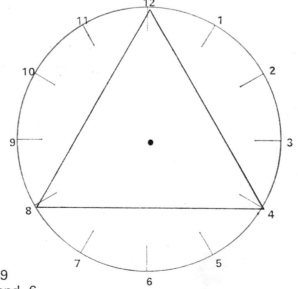

Find what shapes are formed by joining these numbers in order:

(a) 10, 2 and 6   (b) 1, 3, 7 and 9
(c) 12, 7 and 5   (d) 11, 1, 3 and 9
(e) 8, 11, 2 and 5   (f) 10, 12, 2 and 6
(g) 12, 2, 4, 6, 8 and 10   (h) 1, 2, 3, 4, 5, 6, 7, 8, 9, 10, 11, 12

Useful information

Until we go completely metric you will sometimes want to know how metric weights and measures compare with the weights and measures commonly used at present. Here are the approximate equivalents:

Length:
$2\frac{1}{2}$ centimetres — 1 inch

30 centimetres — 1 foot

1 metre — 3 inches more than a yard

1 kilometre — $\frac{5}{8}$ of a mile.

Weight:
1 kilogramme — a little more than 2 lb.

500 grammes — about 1 lb.

Volume:
1 litre — $1\frac{3}{4}$ pints

$4\frac{1}{2}$ litres — 1 gallon

5 millilitres — about a teaspoonful

10 millilitres — about a tablespoonful

Money:

New Money	50p	10p	5p	2p	1p	$\frac{1}{2}$p
Old Money	10/–	2/–	1/–	5d	2d	1d

BRITAIN'S NEW DECIMAL SYSTEM CURRENCY

This reproduction shows the reverse designs of the six new coins, and the obverse design, which is common to all. These are reproduced at twice their diameter size.